Advanced

Programming Techniques

Published by Maia L.L.C.
Idaho, U.S.A.
maiaco.com

ISBN 978-0-9833840-5-2 (e-book)
ISBN 978-0-9833840-2-1 (paper back)

Cover photo: The Cat's Eye Nebula from NASA and the Hubble Space Telescope

Contents

Preface

Learning to program a computer is a frustrating task for many people. In my teaching experience I have found that much of this frustration comes because students are not shown enough programming examples. All of us learn by watching others, so why should learning to program a computer be any different? I wrote this book with minimal text but filled with many computer programming examples to help students and professionals learn computer programming more efficiently and thoroughly with less frustration.

Who Should Read This Book?

I wrote this book for my students graduating with a degree in computer science or information technology from Brigham Young University – Idaho. Consequently, those that will benefit most from reading this book are fourth year undergraduate students, graduate students, and software developers with less than three years of work experience. Each chapter within this book starts with content easily understood by second year undergraduate students and moves quickly to more difficult content. This is my attempt to lure students to study content that is more difficult than they normally would.

How to Use This Book

You can use this book as a tutorial or a reference. When using it as a tutorial, you will find it helpful to step through the example code line by line as if you were a computer. Doing this is sometimes called a *desk check* because you are checking the code on paper or "at your desk" instead of running it on a computer. To aid you in desk checking the example code, I have provided desk check locations throughout the book. Each desk check location includes a list of all the variables found in the corresponding example code and values for the input variables. To perform a desk check, step through the code as if you were the computer and change the value of each variable just as the computer would. The answers to all desk checks are in Appendix B.

Because of the many code examples in this book, you may also use it as a reference where you can find how to correctly implement and use algorithms, including binary search; setting, clearing, and counting bits; converting recursion to iteration and vice versa; computing the intersection, union, and complement of two sets; computing in a numerically stable way the mean and variance of a sample and the correlation of two samples; and much more. All the code examples in this book are written in Java except for those in Chapter 3 Linked Lists, which are written in C.

Acknowledgments

Thank you to my many professors, fellow students, and colleagues for the knowledge they shared with me.

Review This Book

Please write a review of this book at www.amazon.com/dp/B006R2CSXM. Your comments and suggestions help the author and publisher produce better books.

1
Arrays

An *array* is a collection of variables where each variable has the same data type, for example, an array of integers or an array of Appliance objects. Each variable in an array is called an *element* and has an *index*, also called the *subscript*, which denotes that element's location within the array. One advantage of using arrays is that all the elements within an array can be declared, created, and passed to a function as a whole. However, each element may still be accessed individually by using the element's index. Figure 1 shows a representation of an array with 10 elements. Notice that each element has a unique index, and the first index of an array is 0.

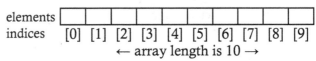

Figure 1: A representation of an array showing the elements and indices.

Fill an Array

It is often desirable to have the computer initialize all the elements in an array to a single value (usually zero). We do this by writing a statement that assigns a value to one element in the array, and then put that assignment statement inside a loop. If the array has *n* elements in it, then the loop causes the computer to repeat the assignment statement *n* times, once for each element in the array.

Example 1

```
/** Fills an array with the value x. */
public static void fill(double[] list, double x) {
    for (int i = 0;  i < list.length;  ++i) {
        list[i] = x;
    }
}
```

Desk Check

list   x   i

8.3

[0] [1] [2] [3]

Within the Java 1.7 libraries, there is already a fill method in the java.util.Arrays class. It is written almost exactly as shown above.

Initialize an Array to a Ramp

Within programs that perform image processing, we often use an array as a *palette*. To get the color value to display for a pixel, the computer reads a pixel value from the image and then looks up that value in the palette. Then the computer displays the color from the palette at the corresponding pixel location on the monitor. Often the palette must be initialized to contain values that are constantly increasing, for example: 0, 1, 2, 3... This is known as a ramp because if you plotted the values in the array, you would see a sloping line or ramp, constantly increasing to the right as shown in Figure 2.

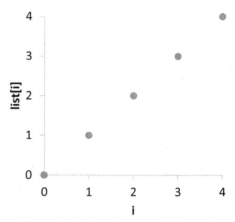

Figure 2: A plot of constantly increasing values forming a discrete ramp function.

Here is a code example showing how to initialize an array to an increasing ramp.

Example 2

```
/** Fills list with constantly increasing values
 * from 0 to list.length - 1, inclusive. */
public static void ramp(int[] list) {
    for (int i = 0;  i < list.length;  ++i) {
        list[i] = i;
    }
}
```

Desk Check

list

[0]	[1]	[2]	[3]	[4]

i

Occasionally we want to initialize an array to hold constantly decreasing values such as: 15, 14, 13, ... 0. This is known as a reverse ramp because if you plotted the values in the array, you would see a sloping line or ramp, constantly decreasing to the right as shown in Figure 3. Example code to initialize an array to a reverse ramp is shown below.

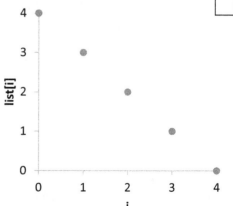

Figure 3: A plot of constantly decreasing values forming a discrete reverse ramp function.

Example 3

```
/** Fills list with constantly decreasing
 * values from list.length - 1 to 0, inclusive. */
public static void reverseRamp(int[] list) {
    int high = list.length - 1;
    for (int i = 0;  i < list.length;  ++i) {
        list[i] = high - i;
    }
}
```

Desk Check

list

[0] [1] [2] [3] [4]

high i

Reverse an Array

Reversing the order of the elements in an array is not commonly used in computer programs. However, it is an interesting operation, and understanding it helps students to understand more commonly used array operations. One way to reverse the elements in an array is to use two index variables: one index starts at the beginning of the array, and the other starts at the end of the array. Then write a loop that repeats *n* / *2* times where *n* is the number of elements in the array. Each time through the loop, the computer switches one element in the left half of the array with one element in the right half.

Example 4

```
/** Reverses the contents of an array. */
public static void reverse(float[] list) {
    int left = 0;
    int right = list.length - 1;
    while (left < right) {
        // Exchange two elements.
        float swap = list[left];
        list[left] = list[right];
        list[right] = swap;

        // Move the indices toward the center.
        left++;
        right--;
    }
}
```

Desk Check

list

3.4	-2	5	7	-12

[0] [1] [2] [3] [4]

left right swap

Rotate an Array

Rotating the elements of an array is also not commonly used in most programs, but is useful to help us study arrays. Rotating the elements of an array one position to the left is easily done by storing the first element in a temporary variable, moving all the other elements one position to the left, and then copying the value from the temporary variable to the last position in the array.

Example 5

```
/** Rotates the elements of an
 * array one position to the left. */
public static void rotateLeft(float[] list) {
    int last = list.length - 1;
    float swap = list[0];
    for (int i = 0;  i < last;  ++i) {
        list[i] = list[i + 1];
    }
    list[last] = swap;
}
```

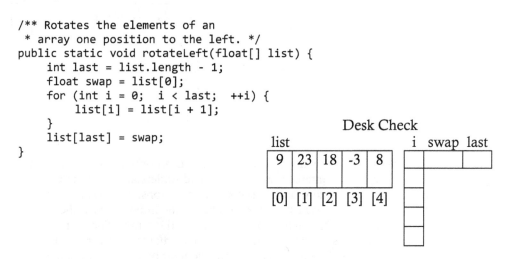

Rotating the elements of an array to the right can be done similarly to rotating to the left except moving each element to the right is done from the end of the array to the beginning.

Example 6

```
/** Rotates the elements in an
 * array one position to the right. */
public static void rotateRight(float[] list) {
    int last = list.length - 1;
    float swap = list[last];
    for (int i = last;  i > 0;  --i) {
        list[i] = list[i - 1];
    }
    list[0] = swap;
}
```

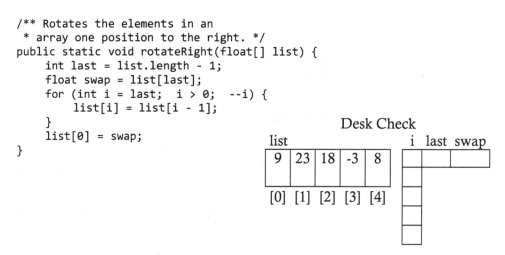

Rotating the elements of an array by more than one position forms groups of elements that trade positions with one another. The number of groups is always the greatest common divisor of the number of positions to rotate and the array length. For example, rotating an array of length 6 two positions to the right forms 2 groups of 3 elements that trade positions as shown in Figure 4.

Before rotating

11	23	−5	9	−3	14
[0]	[1]	[2]	[3]	[4]	[5]

After rotating

−3	14	11	23	−5	9
[0]	[1]	[2]	[3]	[4]	[5]

Figure 4: Rotating an array of 6 elements two positions to the right forms 2 groups of 3 elements each.

Example 7

```
/** Rotates the elements of an array by k positions.
 * Negative values of k rotate to the left.  Positive
 * values rotate to the right. */
public static void rotate(float[] list, int k) {
    int n = list.length;
    k %= n;
    if (k < 0) {  // rotate left
        k = -k;
    }
    else if (k > 0) {  // rotate right
        k = n - k;
    }
    else {  // no rotation
        return;
    }
    int groups = gcd(k, n);
    for (int group = 0;  group < groups;  group++) {
        int one = group;
        int two;
        float save = list[one];
        while ((two = (one + k) % n) != group) {
            list[one] = list[two];
            one = two;
        }
        list[one] = save;
    }
}
```

Desk Check

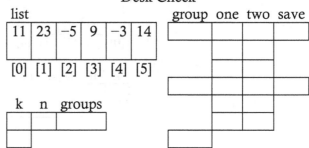

Example 8

```
/** Returns the greatest common divisor of two integers. */
private static int gcd(int a, int b) {
    // Ensure a and b are not negative.
    a = Math.abs(a);
    b = Math.abs(b);

    // Loop until the greatest common divisor is found.
    int r;   // Holds the remainder
    do {
        r = a % b;
        a = b;
        b = r;
    } while (r != 0);
    return a;
}
```

Desk Check

a	b	r	return

It is interesting to note that we don't need to actually rotate the elements of an array in order to process the elements in a rotated order. Consider this code that prints the elements of an array in a rotated order without ever rotating the array.

Example 9

```
/** Prints the elements in an array in a rotated order without
 * actually rotating the contents of the array. Negative k prints
 * with a left rotation and positive k with a right rotation. */
public static void printRotated(float[] list, int k) {
    System.out.print('[');
    final int n = list.length;
    int index = -(k % n);
    if (index < 0)
        index += n;
    String separator = "";
    for (int i = 0;  i < n;  ++i) {
        System.out.print(separator);
        separator = ", ";
        System.out.print(list[index]);
        if (++index == n) {
            index = 0;
        }
    }
    System.out.println(']');
}
```

Desk Check

list

11	23	−5	9	−3	14
[0]	[1]	[2]	[3]	[4]	[5]

k	n	separator

index	i	console output

Advanced Programming Techniques

Linear Search

Very often a computer program must determine if a certain value is stored in an array or not and if stored in the array, then return the value's location. The value to be found is called the *key*. If the array is not too large (perhaps less than 100 elements), finding the key can be easily done using a linear search. A linear search is done by comparing each element in the array with the key until the key is found in the array or the end of the array is reached.

The advantage of a linear search is that it is simple and easy to code. The disadvantage is that it is too slow if the array has many elements in it. When the array has many elements in it, it is likely faster to sort the array and keep it sorted and to use a binary search to find the key within the array.

Java code to perform a linear search is shown below. In the example, if the key is found in the array, the search function returns the index of the location within the array where the key was found. If the key is not found, the search function returns −1.

Example 10

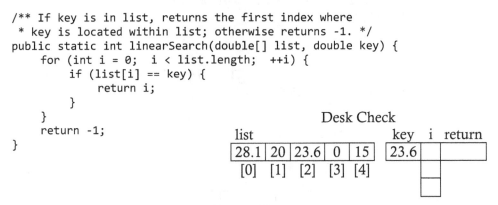

```
/** If key is in list, returns the first index where
 * key is located within list; otherwise returns -1. */
public static int linearSearch(double[] list, double key) {
    for (int i = 0;  i < list.length;  ++i) {
        if (list[i] == key) {
            return i;
        }
    }
    return -1;
}
```

Desk Check

list					key	i	return
28.1	20	23.6	0	15	23.6		
[0]	[1]	[2]	[3]	[4]			

Binary Search

If the elements in an array are sorted, then the computer can use a faster algorithm called *binary search* to find an element within that array. The binary search algorithm works by comparing the key to the middle most element in the array. If the key is greater than the middle most element, then the search is repeated in the last half of the array. If the key is less than the middle most element, then the search is repeated in the first half of the array. Of course, if the key is equal to the middle most element, then the key has been found and the search is done. This process of comparing the key to the middle most element of the current interval is repeated until the key is found or the interval has shrunk to only one element. If that one element is not the same as the key, then the key is not present in the array, and the function below returns a negative value.

Example 11

```
/** If key is in list, returns any index where key is
 * located within list; otherwise returns -insertPoint - 1.
 * Assumes list is already sorted. */
public static int binarySearch(float[] list, float key) {
    int left = 0;
    int right = list.length - 1;
    while (left <= right) {
        int mid = left + ((right - left) >>> 1);
        float cmp = key - list[mid];
        if (cmp > 0) {
            left = mid + 1;
        }
        else if (cmp < 0) {
            right = mid - 1;
        }
        else {
            return mid;
        }
    }

    // key is not present in list, but if it
    // were, it would be stored at location left.
    return -(left + 1);
}
```

Desk Check

list

−2.1	−1	3.9	6.2	7.1	9.7	10	12	13.1	15.6	18	19	20.1	24.5
[0]	[1]	[2]	[3]	[4]	[5]	[6]	[7]	[8]	[9]	[10]	[11]	[12]	[13]

key	left	right	mid	cmp	return
15.6					

If the key is not present in the array, the return value of the binary search function above is −*insertPoint* − 1. In other words, if the key is not present in the array, the index where key should be inserted can be found using this code:

```
int index = binarySearch(list, key);
if (index < 0) {
    int insertPoint = -index - 1;
}
```

In the binarySearch code above, the statement that computes mid needs some explanation. Here is the line:

```
mid = left + ((right - left) >>> 1);
```

The unsigned right shift operator (>>>) shifts all the bits in an integer to the right which is the same as using integer division to divide a **non-negative integer** by a power of two. However, the right shift operator executes faster than integer division. To help us understand the statement, we can rewrite it by replacing >>> 1 with / 2.

```
mid = left + (right - left) / 2;
```

Notice that this statement uses integer division to truncate (not round) the result of the division. Also notice that if this were an algebraic expression, it could be simplified to

```
mid = (left + right) / 2;
```

which is easier to understand. From this simplified formula we see that the midpoint is simply the left index plus the right index divided in half. However, because an array in Java can have as many as 2,147,483,647 ($2^{31} - 1$) elements, and that is also the largest number that an int can hold, we must use the more complex formula.

To understand why we must use the more complex formula, imagine an array with just slightly more than 2^{30} elements, say 1,073,741,829 ($2^{30} + 5$), a little more than 1 gigabyte of elements. Now imagine that the computer is nearing the end of its binary search for some value that is located near the end of the array. What happens with our simplified formula when left = 1,073,741,821 and right = 1,073,741,828? You and I can add those two numbers together to get 2,147,483,649. However, that sum is larger than the largest value that a Java int can hold. So when the computer adds those two numbers together the 32-bit int in the computer's CPU overflows, and the computer gets the sum of −1,073,741,823. Yes, that's right, the computer adds two large positive numbers together and gets a negative number as a result. This is known as *overflow*. Obviously the negative sum is incorrect, and even after it is divided by 2 (see the simplified formula above), it will still be negative and will still cause an ArrayIndexOutOfBoundsException. So, we must use the more complex formula.

Within the Java 1.7 libraries, there is an existing binary search function in the java.util.Arrays class. However, as of Java 1.7 it still uses the simple expression for computing the middle index between left and right:

```
mid = (left + right) >>> 1
```

which is a bug.

Find a Range

Sometimes a computer program has a list of numerical ranges and must find the range that contains some value. Examples of this type of computing problem include:

- determining a person's income tax rate from a list of income ranges and graduated tax rates
- determining a customer's discount rate from a list of purchase ranges and discount rates
- determining a salesperson's commission from a list of sales ranges and commission rates
- determining a student's letter grade from a list of score ranges and letter grades

For example, a company may offer discounts to its customers where the discount rate is based on the amount purchased according to this table.

If the purchase amount is greater than or equal to	And the purchase amount is less than	Then the discount rate is
0	$300	0%
$300	$600	2.0%
$600	$1000	2.5%
$1000	Infinity	3.0%

A beginning programmer will often code a Java solution to this problem like this:

Example 12

```java
/** Computes and returns a discounted purchase amount. */
public static double getDiscountedAmount(double purchase) {
    double rate = 0;
    if (purchase >= 0 && purchase < 300) {
        rate = 0;
    }
    if (purchase >= 300 && purchase < 600) {
        rate = 0.02;
    }
    if (purchase >= 600 && purchase < 1000) {
        rate = 0.025;
    }
    if (purchase >= 1000) {
        rate = 0.03;
    }
    double discount = purchase * rate;
    return purchase - discount;
}
```

Desk Check

purchase	rate	discount	return
$708.00			

After a little practice, the beginning programmer realizes that the separate if statements can be connected with else and that the else part of each if statement will be executed only when the previous if part is false. This means the code can be written more succinctly and achieve exactly the same results by removing the left half of each if statement.

Example 13

```
/** Computes and returns a discounted purchase amount. */
public static double getDiscountedAmount(double purchase) {
    double rate;
    if (purchase < 300) {
        rate = 0;
    } else if (purchase < 600) {
        rate = 0.02;
    } else if (purchase < 1000) {
        rate = 0.025;
    } else {
        rate = 0.03;
    }
    double discount = purchase * rate;
    return purchase - discount;
}
```

Desk Check

purchase	rate	discount	return
$708.00			

The problem with both these solutions is that if the company changes the purchase amount ranges or the discount rates, then a programmer must change the corresponding code. An improved solution is to remove the ranges and rates from the code and place them in a file or database so that the computer can read them into an array or arrays when it runs the program. Then the programmer must write a simple linear or binary search to find the correct range and the corresponding discount rate as shown in the next example.

Example 14

```
// The values in these arrays can be hard coded
// into your program, or even better, they can be
// read from a file or database.
static final double[] limits = { 300, 600, 1000 };
static final double[] rates = { 0, .02, .025, .03 };

/** Computes and returns a discounted purchase amount. */
public static double getDiscountedAmount(double purchase) {
    int i;
    for (i = 0;  i < limits.length;  ++i) {
        if (purchase < limits[i]) {
            break;
        }
    }
    double rate = rates[i];
    double discount = purchase * rate;
    return purchase - discount;
}
```

Desk Check

purchase	i	rate	discount	return
$708.00				

Table Based Solutions

A programming solution like the previous one is known as a *table based* solution because tables of data are stored in arrays instead of being stored in the code inside if statements. A table based solution is almost always shorter and less complex than a corresponding solution that doesn't use tables. Consider the following code that creates a number pad for a Java Swing graphical user interface.

Example 15

```java
private static JPanel makeNumberPad() {
    JButton btnZero  = new JButton("0");
    JButton btnOne   = new JButton("1");
    JButton btnTwo   = new JButton("2");
    JButton btnThree = new JButton("3");
    JButton btnFour  = new JButton("4");
    JButton btnFive  = new JButton("5");
    JButton btnSix   = new JButton("6");
    JButton btnSeven = new JButton("7");
    JButton btnEight = new JButton("8");
    JButton btnNine = new JButton("9");
    JPanel numberPad = new JPanel(new GridLayout(4, 3));
    numberPad.add(btnSeven);
    numberPad.add(btnEight);
    numberPad.add(btnNine);
    numberPad.add(btnFour);
    numberPad.add(btnFive);
    numberPad.add(btnSix);
    numberPad.add(btnOne);
    numberPad.add(btnTwo);
    numberPad.add(btnThree);
    numberPad.add(btnZero);
    return numberPad;
}
```

Now consider this much shorter solution that creates the same number pad but uses a table of Strings to hold the text for all buttons and a loop to create all ten buttons.

Example 16

```java
private static JPanel makeNumberPad() {
    String[] buttonTexts = {
        "7", "8", "9",
        "4", "5", "6",
        "1", "2", "3",
        "0"
    };
    JPanel numberPad = new JPanel(new GridLayout(4, 3));
    for (int i = 0;  i < buttonTexts.length;  i++) {
        JButton button = new JButton(buttonTexts[i]);
        numberPad.add(button);
    }
    return numberPad;
}
```

The table based solution (second example) is preferred because it requires less code. Less code is almost always easier to write, read, and understand, and it usually has fewer mistakes because there is simply less code to contain the mistakes.

Roman Numerals

When you are writing table based solutions, quite often a single table can be used in more than one function. The next function uses a table of Strings stored as a two-dimensional array to convert an Arabic number to Roman numerals. The function after uses the same table to perform the opposite conversion.

Example 17

```
/** The data table used to convert Arabic
 * numbers to Roman numerals and vice versa. */
private static final String[][] numerals = {
    { "", "I", "II", "III", "IV", "V", "VI", "VII", "VIII", "IX" },
    { "", "X", "XX", "XXX", "XL", "L", "LX", "LXX", "LXXX", "XC" },
    { "", "C", "CC", "CCC", "CD", "D", "DC", "DCC", "DCCC", "CM" },
    { "", "M", "MM", "MMM" }
};

/** Converts a base 10 Arabic number to Roman numerals. */
public static String romanFromArabic(int arabic) {
    assert 0 <= arabic && arabic < 4000;
    String roman = "";
    int divisor = 1000;

    // Count down from the thousands
    // column (3) to the ones column (0).
    for (int exponent = 3;  exponent >= 0;  exponent--) {

        // Extract one Arabic digit.
        int digit = arabic / divisor;

        // Look up the corresponding Roman pattern
        // and concatenate it to the Roman numerals.
        roman += numerals[exponent][digit];

        // Subtract the digit from the Arabic number.
        arabic -= digit * divisor;

        // Prepare the divisor for the next column.
        divisor /= 10;
    }
    return roman;
}
```

Desk Check

arabic	exponent	divisor	digit	roman
1987				

Example 18

```
/** Converts Roman numerals to a base 10 Arabic number. */
public static int arabicFromRoman(String roman) {
    int arabic = 0;

    // Count down from the thousands
    // column (3) to the ones column (0).
    for (int exponent = 3;  exponent >= 0;  exponent--) {

        // The longest possible "single digit" Roman
        // pattern has 4 characters, e.g. VIII
        int length = Math.min(roman.length(), 4);

        for (;  length > 0;  length--) {
            // Extract characters from the Roman number.
            String chars = roman.substring(0, length);

            // Find the extracted characters using linear search.
            int digit = linearSearch(numerals[exponent], chars);
            if (digit >= 0) {
                arabic += digit * Math.pow(10, exponent);
                roman = roman.substring(length);
                break;
            }
        }
    }
    return arabic;
}
```

Desk Check

roman	exponent	length	chars	digit	arabic
"MCMLXXXVII"					

Sort an Array

The best way to sort an array is to use the sort functionality provided by the programming language that you are using because this built in sorting functionality has been optimized and tested. Java includes built in sort functionality which is in the java.util.Arrays class. Here is Java code to sort an array using the built in functionality.

Example 19

```
String[] list = { "Radish", "Carrot", "Tomato", "Pea" };
java.util.Arrays.sort(list);
```

In Java, if you wish to sort objects created from your own class, then you must implement and create a Comparator object and pass that Comparator object as the second parameter to Arrays.sort. The sort function will call the compare function in the Comparator object to compare two objects and the compare function will return one of the following:

- a negative integer if the first object should be placed before the second in the sorted array
- a zero (0) if the contents of the two objects are equal
- a positive number if the first object should be placed after the second in the sorted array

Then the sort function will switch the location of the two objects if necessary and repeat this process many times for all elements until the entire array is sorted.

This Java code shows how to sort Student objects by name and by age using two different Comparator objects.

Example 20

```
import java.util.Arrays;
import java.util.Comparator;

public class Student {
    private String name;
    private int age;

    public Student(String name, int age) {
        this.name = name;
        this.age = age;
    }

    @Override
    public String toString() {
        return name + " " + age;
    }
```

```java
    /** A Comparator used when sorting Students by name. */
    static class NameComptor implements Comparator<Student> {
        @Override
        public int compare(Student s1, Student s2) {
            int r = s1.name.compareTo(s2.name);

            // If two students have the same
            // name, order them by their ages.
            if (r == 0) {
                r = s1.age - s2.age;
            }
            return r;
        }
    }


    /** A Comparator used when sorting Students by age. */
    static class AgeComptor implements Comparator<Student> {
        @Override
        public int compare(Student s1, Student s2) {
            int r = s1.age - s2.age;

            // If two students have the same
            // age, order them by their names.
            if (r == 0) {
                r = s1.name.compareTo(s2.name);
            }
            return r;
        }
    }


    public static void main(String[] args) {
        Student[] students = {
            new Student("Jane", 18),
            new Student("Sam", 17),
            new Student("Nigel", 14)
        };
        System.out.println(Arrays.toString(students));

        // Sort the students by name.
        Arrays.sort(students, new NameComptor());
        System.out.println(Arrays.toString(students));

        // Sort the students by age.
        Arrays.sort(students, new AgeComptor());
        System.out.println(Arrays.toString(students));
    }
}
```

Desk Check

students			console output
"Jane" 18	"Sam" 17	"Nigel" 14	
[0]	[1]	[2]	

How Does a Sort Function Work?

You might be wondering how a sort function works. There are many different, well known sort algorithms (selection, exchange, insertion, heap, quick, etc.). They all work by repeatedly comparing elements in an array to other elements in the array and simply moving the elements around within the array. Shown below is Java code to sort an array using the insertion sort algorithm. Insertion sort is a simple and reasonably fast algorithm, although it is usually not as fast as the quick sort algorithm.

Example 21

```
/** Sorts the contents of an array in ascending
 * order using the insertion sort algorithm. */
public static void sort(double[] list) {
    int first = 0;
    int last = list.length - 1;

    for (int i = last - 1;  i >= first;  --i) {
        double swap = list[i];
        int j;
        for (j = i + 1;  j <= last;  ++j) {
            if (swap <= list[j]) {
                break;
            }
            list[j - 1] = list[j];
        }
        list[j - 1] = swap;
    }
}
```

Desk Check

list

| 6 | −8 | 9 | 7 | 0 |
| 6 | −8 | 9 | | |

| 6 | −8 | | | |

| 6 | | 0 | 7 | 9 |

| | | | 7 | 9 |

[0] [1] [2] [3] [4]

first last i swap j

Possible User Input

Most computer programs require user input. User friendly programs maintain a list of possible input values. As the user enters input, these programs show a list of possible values, allowing the user to choose from the list which dramatically reduces the user effort required to enter the input. I call this style of gathering input *possible user input*, and it can be implemented with a sorted list of possible input terms and a binary search as shown in the following code examples.

Notice that the `findAnyCandidate` function uses binary search to find **any** term that starts with the user entered prefix. Then the `findCandidates` function performs two secondary searches to find the first and last terms that start with that prefix. I chose linear search for the two secondary searches in `findCandidates` because the list of possible terms is usually too small to merit using the more complex binary search.

The function `startsWithCompare` is used during the binary search and is somewhat unusual because it determines if a possible term starts with a user entered prefix or if not, if the prefix should come before or after the term. In other words, this comparison function is a combination of the Java `String.startsWith` and `String.compareTo` functions.

```
/** A Bounds object holds the index of the first and
 * last values in a list that start with a prefix. */
public class Bounds {
    public int first, last;

    public Bounds(int first, int last) {
        this.first = first;
        this.last = last;
    }
}
```

Example 22

```
/** Returns the indexes of the first and last items
 * in candidates that start with prefix; returns null
 * if no item in candidates starts with prefix. */
public static Bounds findCandidates(String prefix, String[] candidates){
    Bounds bounds = null;

    // Find any item that starts with prefix.
    int index = findAnyCandidate(prefix, candidates);
    if (index >= 0) {
        // Find the first item that starts with prefix.
        int first = index;
        while (--first >= 0) {
            if (!candidates[first].startsWith(prefix)) {
                break;
            }
        }
        first++;

        // Find the last item that starts with prefix.
        int last = index;
        while (++last < candidates.length) {
            if (!candidates[last].startsWith(prefix)) {
                break;
            }
        }
        last--;

        bounds = new Bounds(first, last);
    }
    return bounds;
}
```

Desk Check

candidates

"cash"	"charity"	"clothing"	"dentist"	"dividend"	"doctor"	"education"
[0]	[1]	[2]	[3]	[4]	[5]	[6]

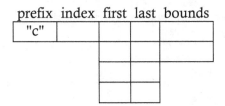

prefix index first last bounds

Example 23

```
/** Returns the index of any item in candidates that starts
 * with prefix; returns -1 if no such item exists. */
private static int findAnyCandidate(String prefix, String[] candidates){
    int left = 0;
    int right = candidates.length - 1;
    while (left <= right) {
        int mid = left + ((right - left) >>> 1);
        String term = candidates[mid];
        int cmp = startsWithCompare(prefix, term);
        if (cmp > 0) {
            left = mid + 1;
        } else if (cmp < 0) {
            right = mid - 1;
        } else {
            return mid;
        }
    }
    return -1;
}
```

Desk Check

candidates

"cash"	"charity"	"clothing"	"dentist"	"dividend"	"doctor"	"education"
[0]	[1]	[2]	[3]	[4]	[5]	[6]

prefix	left	mid	right	term	cmp	return
"c"						

Example 24

```
/** Returns 0 if term starts with prefix; otherwise
 * returns a negative integer if prefix should come
 * before term and a positive integer if prefix
 * should come after term in their normal ordering. */
private static int startsWithCompare(String prefix, String term) {
    int preLen = prefix.length();
    int minLen = Math.min(preLen, term.length());
    for (int i = 0;  i < minLen;  ++i) {
        int diff = prefix.charAt(i) - term.charAt(i);
        if (diff != 0) {
            return diff;
        }
    }
    return preLen == minLen ? 0 : prefix.charAt(minLen);
}
```

Desk Check

prefix	term	preLen	minLen	i	diff	return
"c"	"charity"					

Predictive User Input

Some programs are even smarter and not only maintain a list of possible input values but also a count of how often the user has entered each value. Storing the count enables the program to predict which of the possible values the user is entering. As the user types, the program shows a list of possible values, but the default value is the value that starts with the text the user has entered **and** has been used most often. This allows the user to enter frequently used values even more quickly, and is known as *predictive user input*.

Figure 5 is a screen shot of Ledger 2011, a financial application written using Microsoft Access that employs predictive user input when a user is entering payees, categories, and other information. Notice that the user is entering the data for check #2016 written to the Madison School Lunch program and has typed "Mad" in the Payee column. Because Ledger employs predictive user input for payees, Ledger has predicted that the user is entering "Madison School Lunch" instead of "Madison County" even though Madison County comes before Madison School Lunch in alphabetical order. Ledger predicted Madison School Lunch because the user has entered it more often than she has entered Madison County.

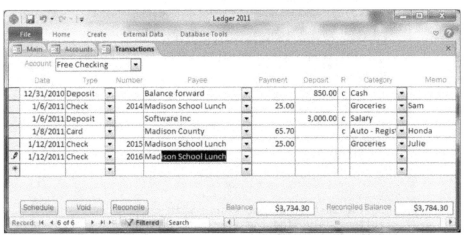

Figure 5: Screen shot of Ledger 2011, a financial application that uses predictive user input. When the user typed "Mad", Ledger predicted Madison School Lunch instead of Madison County because the user has entered Madison School Lunch more often than Madison County.

Here is the Java source code that implements predictive user input to predict which value a user is entering.

```
/** An Entry holds both a possible input value and the
 * number of times that value has been entered by a user. */
class Entry {
    public String term;
    public int uses;  // Number of times term has been used

    public Entry(String term, int uses) {
        this.term = term;
```

```java
        this.uses = uses;
    }

    @Override
    public String toString() {
        return term + ", " + uses;
    }
}
```

Example 25

```java
/** Returns the location of the most frequently used
 * term in candidates that starts with prefix. */
public static int findBestCandidate(String prefix, Entry[] candidates) {
    int index = findAnyCandidate(prefix, candidates);
    if (index >= 0) {
        int max = candidates[index].uses;
        int save = index;

        // Find the first item that starts with prefix, and
        // simultaneously find the item between the first
        // and the one at save that has been used the most.
        int i = save;
        while (--i >= 0) {
            if (candidates[i].term.startsWith(prefix)) {
                int freq = candidates[i].uses;
                if (freq >= max) {
                    max = freq;
                    index = i;
                }
            }
            else {
                break;
            }
        }

        // Find the last item that starts with prefix, and
        // simultaneously find the item between the first
        // and the last one that has been used most often.
        i = save;
        while (++i < candidates.length) {
            if (candidates[i].term.startsWith(prefix)) {
                int freq = candidates[i].uses;
                if (freq > max) {
                    max = freq;
                    index = i;
                }
            }
            else {
                break;
            }
        }
    }
    return index;
}
```

Desk Check

candidates

"cash"	"charity"	"clothing"	"dentist"	"dividend"	"doctor"	"education"
17	8	6	7	14	11	4
[0]	[1]	[2]	[3]	[4]	[5]	[6]

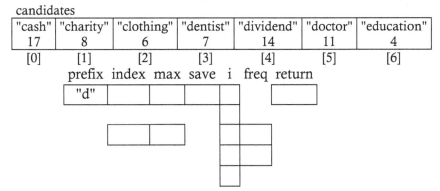

prefix index max save i freq return

Example 26

```java
/** Returns the index of any item in candidates that starts
 * with prefix.  Returns -1 if no such item exists. */
private static int findAnyCandidate(String prefix, Entry[] candidates) {
    int left = 0;
    int right = candidates.length - 1;
    while (left <= right) {
        int mid = left + ((right - left) >>> 1);
        String term = candidates[mid].term;
        int cmp = startsWithCompare(prefix, term);
        if (cmp > 0) {
            left = mid + 1;
        } else if (cmp < 0) {
            right = mid - 1;
        } else {
            return mid;
        }
    }
    return -1;
}
```

Desk Check

candidates

"cash"	"charity"	"clothing"	"dentist"	"dividend"	"doctor"	"education"
17	8	6	7	14	11	4
[0]	[1]	[2]	[3]	[4]	[5]	[6]

prefix left mid right term cmp return

"d"						

Programming Exercises

1. Rewrite the getDiscountedAmount function in example 14 to use a binary search to find the correct range instead of a linear search.

2. Download, install, and use Ledger 2011 to really understand how much easier it is to enter data when the computer correctly predicts what you are trying to enter.

2
Array Lists

An *array list* (or *vector* as it is sometimes called) is an abstract data structure that holds a list of values in an array. In C++, the standard template library (STL) vector can hold pointers and primitive variables, such as int and double. In Java the ArrayList and Vector collections can hold only references to Objects, not primitive variables. However, in Java both StringBuffer and StringBuilder are essentially array lists that contain characters. Array lists normally provide the following very useful methods:

- add - Appends an element at the end of the list.
- insert - Inserts an element at the beginning or in the middle of the list.
- size - Returns how many elements are in the list.
- get - Returns the element at a specified location.
- find - Returns the location of a specified element.
- remove - Removes an element from the list.

Internally, array lists have an array with the elements stored at the beginning of the array and extra space at the end of the array. The entire length of the array is known as the array list's *capacity*, and the actual number of elements stored in the array is known as the array list's *size*. While adding elements, the extra space at the end of the array gradually fills up, meaning the size becomes equal to the capacity. If the array is full when a program computer adds another element to it, the code for the array list will cause the computer to

1. Create a new larger array
2. Copy the contents of the old array to the new larger one
3. Discard the old array
4. Add the element to the new larger array

Initial Capacity and Quantum

Whenever a programmer implements an array list, two important questions arise.

1. How big should the initial array be? This is called the *initial capacity*.
2. When the array needs to grow, by how much should its capacity grow? This is known as the *quantum* and can be constant, such as 20, or variable, for example double the capacity.

Figure 6 shows an array list with an initial capacity of eight elements that was full with the characters "Wonderfu". The program called the add method to add the character "l", so the computer increased the array list's capacity by six elements and then added the "l" to the new larger array within the array list.

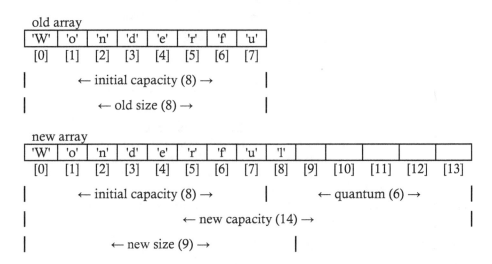

Figure 6: A representation of an array list that was full, and the computer increased its capacity and added another element.

It is difficult to choose a good constant quantum, and a constant quantum is usually inefficient in either compute time or memory space. If a programmer chooses a small constant quantum, such as 8, and a program adds thousands of elements several at a time to the array list, the computer will waste a lot of time repeatedly creating a new larger array and copying the contents of the old array to the new one. If the programmer chooses a large constant quantum, and a program adds only a few elements to the array list, the array list will contain a lot of empty, wasted space at the end.

A variable quantum, such as doubling the capacity each time the array list needs to grow, eliminates much of the wasted compute time because as the array list grows so does the quantum, resulting in far less array creating and copying. However, doubling the size of an array easily leads to wasted memory space. Consider an empty `StringBuilder` that begins with a capacity of 16 characters. Now assume the computer adds 513 characters, several characters at a time. The `StringBuilder` will first double its capacity to 32 characters, then 64, then 128, then 256, then 512, and finally to a capacity of 1024 characters. However, the `StringBuilder` will have only 513 characters stored in it, resulting in 511 characters of wasted space.

The following table shows the initial capacities and quantums for several Java classes that use array lists.

Initial Capacity and Quantum of Java Lists

Data Structure	Initial Capacity	Quantum
ArrayList	10 references	1.5 times the current capacity
Vector	10 references	a programmer specified amount, or if not specified, twice the current capacity
StringBuffer	16 chars	twice the current capacity
StringBuilder	16 chars	twice the current capacity

Advanced Programming Techniques

Fibonacci Variable Quantum

A nice compromise between a fixed quantum and the doubling variable quantum is a variable quantum that follows a Fibonacci series. A Fibonacci series, named after an Italian mathematician, is a series of numbers where each number is the sum of the previous two numbers. Of course, the first two numbers in the series must be given. The classic Fibonacci series starts with 0 and 1: 0, 1, 1, 2, 3, 5, 8... However, we can start a Fibonacci series with any two numbers we choose. Consider the series that begins with 4 and 8: 4, 8, 12, 20, 32, 52... Every number in this series is a multiple of 4. Most memory allocation functions, including `malloc` and `new` allocate memory in chunks whose size are multiples of 4. Even if you write code that asks for 7 bytes, the memory allocation function will probably allocate 8 bytes. So, if we use a Fibonacci series that contains only multiples of 4 as our variable quantum, we can eliminate some wasted bytes in our program.

It is interesting to plot the capacity of array lists that use a different quantum to see how the capacity grows over time. Figure 7 shows a graph of the capacity of four array lists that each uses a different quantum:

1. A fixed quantum of 12 elements
2. A variable quantum that is 1.5 times the previous capacity
3. A Fibonacci variable quantum that begins with 12 and 20
4. A variable quantum that is 2 times the previous capacity

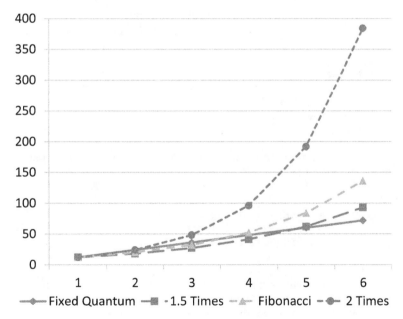

Figure 7: A graph of the capacity of array lists that use four different quantums.

From the graph we see how slowly the capacity of an array list with a fixed quantum grows over time which usually results in lots of wasted computer time allocating larger arrays and copying data. We also see how quickly the capacity of an array list with a 2 times variable quantum grows which often results in wasted memory space. The Fibonacci variable quantum is a nice compromise between the fixed quantum and the 2 times variable quantum.

Memory Efficient StringBuilder

As shown in the previous table, the Java StringBuilder class uses a double variable quantum. We can write our own StringBuilder class as shown in Figure 8 and the example code below that uses the more memory efficient Fibonacci series as the quantum. In the code below notice the four append methods call the ensureCapacity method which calls expandCapacity if necessary. expandCapacity calls findFibonacci which chooses the new larger capacity by finding the smallest Fibonacci number that is greater than or equal to the suggested capacity.

StringBuilder
−FIBS : int[]
−array : char[]
−count : int
+StringBuilder()
+StringBuilder(capacity : int)
+length() : int
+charAt(index : int) : char
+toString() : String
+append(c : char) : StringBuilder
+append(a : char[]) : StringBuilder
+append(sb : StringBuilder) : StringBuilder
+append(s : String) : StringBuilder
+ensureCapacity(capacity : int) : void
#expandCapacity(suggest : int) : void
−findFibonacci(value : int) : int

Figure 8: A UML class diagram for a StringBuilder class that uses a Fibonacci variable quantum.

```
/** A mutable sequence of characters.  You can think of
 * a string builder as a string that can be modified. */
public class StringBuilder {
    /** An array to store the character data. */
    char[] array;

    /** Actual number of characters stored in the array */
    int count;


    /** Constructs a string builder with no characters
     * in it and an initial capacity of 12 characters. */
    public StringBuilder() { this(12); }


    /** Constructs a string builder with no characters
     * in it and the specified initial capacity. */
    public StringBuilder(int capacity) {
        capacity = findFibonacci(capacity);
        array = new char[capacity];
        count = 0;
    }
}
```

```
/** Returns the number of characters
 * stored in this StringBuilder. */
public int length() { return count; }
```

```
/** Returns the character stored in this
 * StringBuilder at the specified index. */
public char charAt(int index) { return array[index]; }
```

```
@Override
public String toString() {
    return new String(array, 0, count);
}
```

Example 1

```
/** Appends a single character to this StringBuilder. */
public StringBuilder append(char c) {
    ensureCapacity(count + 1);
    array[count++] = c;
    return this;
}
```

Desk Check

this.array				this.count	c
'U'	'n'			2	'd'
[0]	[1]	[2]	[3]		

Example 2

```
/** Appends the contents of an array of
 * characters to this StringBuilder. */
public StringBuilder append(char[] a) {
    ensureCapacity(count + a.length);
    for (int i = 0;  i < a.length;  ++i) {
        array[count++] = a[i];
    }
    return this;
}
```

Desk Check

this.array								this.count	i
'U'	'n'	'd'						3	
[0]	[1]	[2]	[3]	[4]	[5]	[6]	[7]		

a		
'a'	'u'	'n'
[0]	[1]	[2]

Example 3

```
/** Appends the contents of another
 * StringBuilder to this StringBuilder. */
public StringBuilder append(StringBuilder sb) {
    ensureCapacity(count + sb.count);
    for (int i = 0;  i < sb.count;  ++i) {
        array[count++] = sb.array[i];
    }
    return this;
}
```

Desk Check

this.array

'U'	'n'	'd'					
[0]	[1]	[2]	[3]	[4]	[5]	[6]	[7]

this.count	i
3	

sb.array

'a'	'u'	'n'	
[0]	[1]	[2]	[3]

sb.count
3

Example 4

```
/** Appends the contents of a
 * String to this StringBuilder. */
public StringBuilder append(String s) {
    int len = s.length();
    int newLen = count + len;
    ensureCapacity(newLen);
    s.getChars(0, len, array, count);
    count = newLen;
    return this;
}
```

Desk Check

this.array

'U'	'n'	'd'	'a'	'u'	'n'						
[0]	[1]	[2]	[3]	[4]	[5]	[6]	[7]	[8]	[9]	[10]	[11]

this.count
6

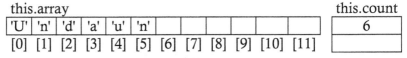

s   newLen

"ted"	

```
/** Ensures the capacity of this
 * StringBuilder is greater than or
 * equal to the specified capacity. */
public void ensureCapacity(int capacity) {
    if (array.length < capacity) {
        expandCapacity(capacity);
    }
}
```

Example 5

```
/** Expands the capacity of this StringBuilder. */
protected void expandCapacity(int suggest) {
    int capacity = findFibonacci(suggest);
    char[] old = array;
    array = new char[capacity];
    System.arraycopy(old, 0, array, 0, count);
}
```

Desk Check

old				this.count	suggest	capacity
'U'	'n'	'd'		3	6	
[0]	[1]	[2]	[3]			

this.array

[0]	[1]	[2]	[3]	[4]	[5]	[6]	[7]

Example 6

```
/** Finds the Fibonacci number greater than or equal to value. */
private static int findFibonacci(int value) {
    int index = java.util.Arrays.binarySearch(FIBS, value);
    if (index < 0) {
        index = -(index + 1);
    }
    return FIBS[index];
}
```

Desk Check

value	index	return
6		

```
/** The Fibonacci series that begins with 4 and 8. */
private static final int[] FIBS = {
    4, 8, 12, 20,
    32, 52, 84, 136,
    220, 356, 576, 932,
    1508, 2440, 3948, 6388,
    10336, 16724, 27060, 43784,
    70844, 114628, 185472, 300100,
    485572, 785672, 1271244, 2056916,
    3328160, 5385076, 8713236, 14098312,
    22811548, 36909860, 59721408, 96631268,
    156352676, 252983944, 409336620, 662320564,
    1071657184, 1733977748, Integer.MAX_VALUE
};
}
```

Programming Exercises

1. Add to the StringBuilder class in this chapter an insert method that inserts a single character at the beginning of the string builder's array.
2. Add to the StringBuilder class in this chapter an insert method that inserts a String at any position in the string builder's array.

3
Linked Lists

A *linked list* is a flexible abstract data structure that is useful for relatively short lists where items are frequently added and removed from the list. Figure 9 shows a non-circular singly linked list that contains three nodes. Because of today's modern programming libraries such as the C++ standard template library (STL) and the Java collections found in the package java.util, few programmers need to write a linked list. However, there are still some programmers that are required to write them, most notably students, library developers, and kernel developers.

Figure 9: A non-circular singly linked list containing three nodes.

A linked list is made up of connected nodes. In C and C++ the nodes are connected using pointers, and in Java and other languages that don't have pointers, the nodes are connected using references. The example code in this chapter is written in C because example 3 in this chapter uses the address of pointers or in other words, pointers to pointers which is not possible in Java.

Inefficient Node Centric Lists

Most programmers would consider writing a linked list, singly or doubly linked, circular or non-circular, as trivial. Unfortunately, almost all programmers write linked lists inefficiently and incorrectly because they are never taught the correct way to write one. Computer programmers are almost always taught to visualize a linked list in a node centric way. In other words, they are taught to focus on the nodes when writing code to add, find, and remove elements from a linked list, which results in C code for a non-circular singly linked list as shown in Figure 10 and example 1.

LinkedNode
−next : LinkedNode *
which : int
+createNode(which : int) : LinkedNode *
+freeNode(node : LinkedNode *) : void

LinkedList
−head : LinkedNode *
−tail : LinkedNode *
+createList() : LinkedList *
+freeList(list : LinkedList *) : void
+listIsEmpty(list : LinkedList *) : int
+getNode(list : LinkedList *, index : int) : LinkedNode *
+findNode(list : LinkedList *, key : int) : LinkedNode *
+insertNode(list : LinkedList *, node : LinkedNode *) : void
+appendNode(list : LinkedList *, node : LinkedNode *) : void
+removeFirst(list : LinkedList *) : LinkedNode *
+removeNode(list : LinkedList *, node : LinkedNode *) : void

Figure 10: A UML class diagram for a node centric singly linked list.

Example 1

```
typedef struct slnode {
    struct slnode *next;
    /* Programmer defined data goes here. */
    int which;
} LinkedNode;

/* Creates and returns a singly-linked node. */
LinkedNode *createNode(int which) {
    LinkedNode *node = malloc(sizeof(*node));
    node->next = NULL;
    node->which = which;
    return node;
}

/* Frees a node. */
void freeNode(LinkedNode *node) {
    node->next = NULL;
    free(node);
}

typedef struct sllist {
    LinkedNode *head, *tail;
} LinkedList;

/* Creates and initializes a non-circular, singly-linked list. */
LinkedList *createList(void) {
    LinkedList *list = malloc(sizeof(*list));
    list->head = NULL;
    list->tail = NULL;
    return list;
}
```

Advanced Programming Techniques

```c
/* Frees all the nodes in this list. */
void freeList(LinkedList *list) {
    LinkedNode *prev, *curr = list->head;
    while ((prev = curr) != NULL) {
        curr = curr->next;
        freeNode(prev);
    }
    list->head = NULL;
    list->tail = NULL;
    free(list);
}

/* Returns true if this list is empty; otherwise returns false. */
int listIsEmpty(const LinkedList *list) {
    return list->head == NULL;
}


/* Returns a pointer to the node in this list at
 * location index or NULL if no such node exists. */
LinkedNode *getNode(const LinkedList *list, int index) {
    LinkedNode *curr = list->head;
    while (curr != NULL) {
        if (index == 0) {
            break;
        }
        --index;
        curr = curr->next;
    }
    return curr;
}


/* Returns a pointer to the node in this list that
 * contains key or NULL if no such node exists. */
LinkedNode *findNode(const LinkedList *list, int key) {
    LinkedNode *curr = list->head;
    while (curr != NULL) {
        if (curr->which == key) {
            break;
        }
        curr = curr->next;
    }
    return curr;
}


/* Inserts a node at the beginning of this list. */
void insertNode(LinkedList *list, LinkedNode *node) {
    if (listIsEmpty(list)) {
        list->tail = node;
    }
    node->next = list->head;
    list->head = node;
}
```

```c
/* Appends a node at the end of this list. */
void appendNode(LinkedList *list, LinkedNode *node) {
    if (listIsEmpty(list)) {
        list->head = node;
    }
    else {
        list->tail->next = node;
    }
    list->tail = node;
    node->next = NULL;
}

/* Removes and returns the first node from this list. */
LinkedNode *removeFirst(LinkedList *list) {
    LinkedNode *first = list->head;
    if (!listIsEmpty(list)) {
        LinkedNode *next = first->next;
        list->head = next;
        if (next == NULL) {
            /* There was only one node in this list.  Now
             * that we are removing it, this list is empty. */
            list->tail = NULL;
        }
        first->next = NULL;
    }
    return first;
}

/* Removes a node from this list. */
void removeNode(LinkedList *list, LinkedNode *node) {
    LinkedNode *prev = list->head;
    if (prev == node) {
        /* The node to be removed is at the beginning
         * of the list.  Remove the node. */
        removeFirst(list);
    }
    else {
        /* Traverse the list to find the node that
         * comes before the one to be removed. */
        while (prev != NULL) {
            if (prev->next == node) {
                /* We found the node, so remove it. */
                LinkedNode *next = node->next;
                prev->next = next;
                if (next == NULL) {
                    /* We are removing the node at the end
                     * of the list, so change the tail. */
                    list->tail = prev;
                }
                node->next = NULL;
                break;
            }
            prev = prev->next;
        }
    }
}
```

Notice the complexity of the appendNode and removeNode functions, especially the removeNode function which even includes a call to the removeFirst function. Because we have taken a node centric approach when writing this linked list, we must write if statements to handle two special cases: when the list is empty and when the node to be removed is at the beginning of the list. The complexity of this code, especially the remove function makes it difficult to code correctly and to test completely.

Dummy Node

Many programmers will reduce the complexity of the append and remove functions by adding an empty dummy node at the beginning of the list. This dummy node contains no user defined data and serves only as a place holder. Figure 11 shows two non-circular singly linked lists that use dummy nodes at the beginning of the list. The first list is empty, and the second contains three nodes with data. Adding a dummy node reduces the complexity of the append and remove functions but slightly increases the complexity of the other functions, and the dummy node wastes some memory. The example code below is an implementation of a non-circular singly linked list with a dummy node at the beginning of the list. Only the functions that differ from example 1 are listed and each differing line is highlighted in bold font.

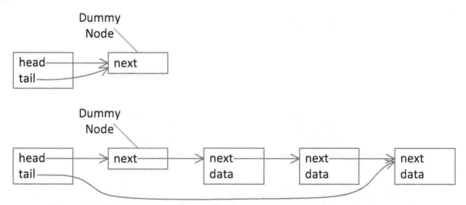

Figure 11: Two non-circular singly linked lists, each with a dummy node.

Example 2

```
/* Creates and initializes a non-circular, singly-linked list
 * with a dummy node at the beginning. */
LinkedList *createList(void) {
    LinkedList *list = malloc(sizeof(*list));
    list->head = createNode(-1);  /* Create the dummy node. */
    list->tail = list->head;
    return list;
}

/* Returns true if this list is empty; otherwise returns false. */
int listIsEmpty(const LinkedList *list) {
    return list->head->next == NULL;
}
```

```
/* Returns a pointer to the node in this list at
 * location index or NULL if no such node exists. */
LinkedNode *getNode(const LinkedList *list, int index) {
    LinkedNode *curr = list->head->next;
    while (curr != NULL) {
        if (index == 0) {
            break;
        }
        --index;
        curr = curr->next;
    }
    return curr;
}



/* Returns a pointer to the node in this list that
 * contains key or NULL if no such node exists. */
LinkedNode *findNode(const LinkedList *list, int key) {
    LinkedNode *curr = list->head->next;
    while (curr != NULL) {
        if (curr->which == key) {
            break;
        }
        curr = curr->next;
    }
    return curr;
}



/* Inserts a node at the beginning of this list. */
void insertNode(LinkedList *list, LinkedNode *node) {
    if (listIsEmpty(list)) {
        list->tail = node;
    }
    LinkedNode *head = list->head;
    node->next = head->next;
    head->next = node;
}



/* Appends a node at the end of this list. */
void appendNode(LinkedList *list, LinkedNode *node) {
    list->tail->next = node;
    list->tail = node;
    node->next = NULL;
}
```

```
/* Removes a node from this list. */
void removeNode(LinkedList *list, LinkedNode *node) {
    /* Traverse the list to find the node that
     * comes before the one to be removed. */
    LinkedNode *prev = list->head;
    LinkedNode *curr = prev->next;
    while (curr != NULL) {
        if (curr == node) {
            /* We found the node, so remove it. */
            LinkedNode *next = node->next;
            prev->next = next;
            if (next == NULL) {
                /* We are removing the node at the end
                 * of the list, so change the tail. */
                list->tail = prev;
            }
            node->next = NULL;
            break;
        }
        prev = curr;
        curr = curr->next;
    }
}


/* Removes and returns the first node from this list. */
LinkedNode *removeFirst(LinkedList *list) {
    LinkedNode *first = list->head->next;
    if (!listIsEmpty(list)) {
        removeNode(list, first);
    }
    return first;
}
```

Elegant and Efficient Pointer Centric Lists

The correct way to write a singly linked list is to visualize the list in a pointer centric
way, focusing on the links (pointers) between the nodes instead of focusing on the
nodes. Pointer centric thinking results in code that uses the address of the head
pointer and next pointers. Such code uses no dummy node, requires less special
case handling, is easier to test because it has fewer paths through the code, and
executes slightly faster than node centric code. Figure 12 shows a non-circular
singly linked list that contains three nodes. Figure 13 and example 3 show an
implementation of a non-circular singly linked list using pointer centric code. Only
the functions that
differ from
example 1 are
listed below and
each differing line
is highlighted in
bold font.

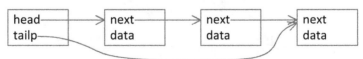

Figure 12: A non-circular singly linked list.

LinkedList
–head : LinkedNode * **–tailp : LinkedNode ****
+createList() : LinkedList * +freeList(list : LinkedList *) : void +listIsEmpty(list : LinkedList *) : int +getNode(list : LinkedList *, index : int) : LinkedNode * +findNode(list : LinkedList *, key : int) : LinkedNode * +insertNode(list : LinkedList *, node : LinkedNode *) : void +appendNode(list : LinkedList *, node : LinkedNode *) : void +removeFirst(list : LinkedList *) : LinkedNode * +removeNode(list : LinkedList *, node : LinkedNode *) : void

Example 3

Figure 13: A UML class diagram for a pointer centric singly linked list.

```
typedef struct sllist {
    LinkedNode *head, **tailp;
} LinkedList;

/* Creates and initializes a non-circular, singly-linked list. */
LinkedList *createList(void) {
    LinkedList *list = malloc(sizeof(*list));
    list->head = NULL;
    list->tailp = &list->head;
    return list;
}

/* Frees all the nodes in this list. */
void freeList(LinkedList *list) {
    LinkedNode *prev, *curr = list->head;
    while ((prev = curr) != NULL) {
        curr = curr->next;
        freeNode(prev);
    }
    list->head = NULL;
    list->tailp = NULL;
    free(list);
}

/* Inserts a node at the beginning of this list. */
void insertNode(LinkedList *list, LinkedNode *node) {
    if (listIsEmpty(list)) {
        list->tailp = &node->next;
    }
    node->next = list->head;
    list->head = node;
}

/* Appends a node at the end of this list. */
void appendNode(LinkedList *list, LinkedNode *node) {
    *list->tailp = node;
    list->tailp = &node->next;
    node->next = NULL;
}
```

```
/* Removes a node from this list. */
void removeNode(LinkedList *list, LinkedNode *node) {
    /* Traverse the list to find the next pointer of the
     * node that comes before the one to be removed. */
    LinkedNode *curr, **pnp = &list->head;
    while ((curr = *pnp) != NULL) {
        if (curr == node) {
            /* We found the node, so remove it. */
            *pnp = node->next;
            if (list->tailp == &node->next) {
                /* We are removing the node at the end
                 * of the list, so change the tail. */
                list->tailp = pnp;
            }
            node->next = NULL;
            break;
        }
        pnp = &curr->next;
    }
}

/* Removes and returns the first node from this list. */
LinkedNode *removeFirst(LinkedList *list) {
    LinkedNode *first = list->head;
    if (first != NULL) {
        removeNode(list, first);
    }
    return first;
}
```

Notice that the appendNode and removeNode functions are much less complex when using a pointer centric approach (example 3). You may be thinking, "The node centric approach (example 1) would not be so complex if you used a circular list or if you wrote it in C++ instead of C." Try it. No matter what you try, if you need to implement a singly linked list with append and remove functions, the pointer centric approach (example 3) will always be less complex.

It is helpful to see why the pointer centric approach is less complex. Notice within the pointer centric LinkedList structure that tailp is a double pointer so that it can hold the address of the head pointer or next pointer within the last node in the list. Consider this C code which creates a linked list and appends three nodes to it.

Example 4

```
1  int main(void) {
2      LinkedList *list = createList();
3      appendNode(list, createNode(1));
4      appendNode(list, createNode(2));
5      appendNode(list, createNode(3));
6      freeList(list);
7      return 0;
8  }
```

Figure 14 shows a representation of the linked list in the computer's memory after line 2 in example 4 is executed. Notice the linked list has been created but is empty because `list->head` is `NULL` and `list->tailp` points to `list->head`.

Memory Address	Variable Name	Value
0x2000	list->head	0x0
0x2008	list->tailp	0x2000

Figure 14: A representation of the contents of the computer's memory after line 2 in example 4 has been executed.

Figure 15 shows the linked list after line 3 has been executed and one node has been added to the list. `list->head` now points to `node1`, and `list->tailp` points to `node1->next`, which is where the next node will be added. This is what makes the `appendNode` function so simple to write. When `node2` is appended to the list, the first line of code in `appendNode`:

Memory Address	Variable Name	Value
0x2000	list->head	0x2010
0x2008	list->tailp	0x2010
0x2010	node1->next	0x0
0x2018	node1->which	1

Figure 15: A representation of the contents of the computer's memory after one node has been added to the list.

```
*list->tailp = node;
```

changes the value in `node1->next` to point at `node2`. Then the second line in `appendNode`:

```
list->tailp = &node->next;
```

changes `tailp` to point at `node2->next` in preparation for another node to be added to the list. This line of code with the ampersand (&) deserves some explanation. The ampersand is the *address-of operator*, so the line is assigning to `tailp` the address of the next field within the last node. This assignment does not require the computer to read any data from memory. Instead it requires the computer to compute the address of the next field within a node by simply adding the offset of the next field to the address of the start of its node. However, in all the example code in this chapter, the offset of the next field is 0 bytes within the `LinkedNode` structure, and so the line:

```
list->tailp = &node->next;
```

doesn't even require addition. For the computer it is a simple assignment like this:

```
list->tailp = (LinkedNode **)node;
```

It is interesting to learn that the C statement without the address-of operator requires the computer to do more work than the C statement that includes the address-of operator. The statement without the address-of operator:

```
curr = curr->next;
```

requires the computer to

1. Add the offset of next (0 in this example) to the address stored in curr.
2. Read from memory the address stored at the address computed in step 1.
3. Store that address in curr.

The statement with the address-of operator:

```
pnp = &curr->next;
```

requires the computer to

1. Add the offset of next (0 in this example) to the address stored in curr.
2. Store that address in pnp.

Figure 16 shows the linked list after line 4 has been executed and two nodes have been added to the list. Notice that list->tailp now contains the address of node2->next. In other words, list->tailp points to node2->next.

Memory Address	Variable Name	Value
0x2000	list->head	0x2010
0x2008	list->tailp	0x2020
0x2010	node1->next	0x2020
0x2018	node1->which	1
0x2020	node2->next	0x0
0x2028	node2->which	2

Figure 16: A representation of the contents of the computer's memory after two nodes have been added to the list.

Figure 17 shows the linked list after line 5 has been executed and all three nodes have been added to the list. list->head still points to node1. Of course node1->next points to node2 and node2->next points to node3. list->tailp points to node3->next which is where the next node will be added to the list.

It is important to remember that the nodes of a linked list do not have to be allocated and stored sequentially in memory as they are in this simple example. Instead the nodes may be scattered throughout memory in a random order, but the next pointers link the nodes together in the order that they were added to the list.

Memory Address	Variable Name	Value
0x2000	list->head	0x2010
0x2008	list->tailp	0x2030
0x2010	node1->next	0x2020
0x2018	node1->which	1
0x2020	node2->next	0x2030
0x2028	node2->which	2
0x2030	node3->next	0x0
0x2038	node3->which	3

Figure 17: A representation of the contents of the computer's memory after three nodes have been added to the list.

Other Data Structures with Pointers

Pointer centric code also works well with other data structures that use pointers. Consider this node centric C code to add a node to a binary search tree. Notice the special case code that is executed when a tree is empty. Special case code is the hallmark of node centric code.

Example 5

```
/** Adds a node to a binary search tree. */
void addNode(BinaryTree *tree, BinaryNode *node) {
    BinaryNode *curr = tree->root;
    if (curr == NULL) {
        /* This tree is empty so add node as its root. */
        tree->root = node;
    }
    else {
        BinaryNode *parent;
        int cmp;

        /* Find within this tree, the node that
         * should be the parent of node. */
        do {
            parent = curr;
            cmp = node->which - parent->which;
            if (cmp < 0) {
                curr = parent->left;
            }
            else if (cmp > 0) {
                curr = parent->right;
            }
            else {
                return;  /* Don't allow duplicate nodes. */
            }
        } while (curr != NULL);

        /* parent now points to the node that should be
         * the parent of node.  So just add node. */
        if (cmp < 0) {
            parent->left = node;
        }
        else if (cmp > 0) {
            parent->right = node;
        }
    }
    node->left = node->right = NULL;
}
```

Now consider this pointer centric code that also adds a node to a binary search tree. Notice how much shorter and simpler it is than the node centric code in the previous example.

Example 6

```
/** Adds a node to a binary search tree. */
void addNode(BinaryTree *tree, BinaryNode *node) {
    BinaryNode *curr, **p = &tree->root;
    while ((curr = *p) != NULL) {
        int cmp = node->which - curr->which;
        if (cmp < 0) {
            p = &curr->left;
        }
        else if (cmp > 0) {
            p = &curr->right;
        }
        else {
            return;  /* Don't allow duplicate nodes. */
        }
    }

    /* p now points to the pointer where node
     * must be added.  So just add node. */
    *p = node;
    node->left = node->right = NULL;
}
```

Doubly Linked List

The most efficient way to write a doubly linked list seems to be to use a dummy node at the beginning of the list. This dummy node holds no user defined data, but instead holds pointers to the first and last nodes in the list. When the list is empty, both of these pointers point to the dummy node itself. Figure 18 shows two non-circular doubly linked lists. The first list is empty, and the second contains three nodes with data. Figure 19 shows a UML class diagram for a doubly linked list and its nodes, and the C code is listed in example 7.

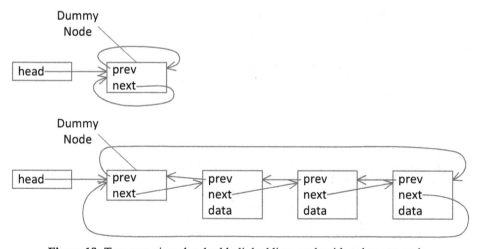

Figure 18: Two non-circuclar doubly linked lists, each with a dummy node.

LinkedNode
−prev : LinkedNode *
−next : LinkedNode *
which : int
+createNode(which : int) : LinkedNode *
+freeNode(node : LinkedNode *) : void

LinkedList
−head : LinkedNode *
+createList() : LinkedList *
+freeList(list : LinkedList *) : void
+listIsEmpty(list : LinkedList *) : int
+getNode(list : LinkedList *, index : int) : LinkedNode *
+findNode(list : LinkedList *, key : int) : LinkedNode *
+insertNode(list : LinkedList *, node : LinkedNode *) : void
+appendNode(list : LinkedList *, node : LinkedNode *) : void
+removeNode(list : LinkedList *, node : LinkedNode *) : void

Figure 19: A UML class diagram for a doubly linked list.

Example 7

```
typedef struct dlnode {
    struct dlnode *prev;
    struct dlnode *next;
    /* Programmer defined data goes here. */
    int which;
} LinkedNode;

/* Creates and returns a doubly-linked node. */
LinkedNode *createNode(int which) {
    LinkedNode *node = malloc(sizeof(*node));
    node->prev = node->next = NULL;
    node->which = which;
    return node;
}

/* Frees a node. */
void freeNode(LinkedNode *node) {
    node->prev = node->next = NULL;
    free(node);
}


typedef struct dllist {
    /* head points to a dummy node at the beginning of the list. */
    LinkedNode *head;

    /* These two pointers are the dummy
     * node at the beginning of the list. */
    LinkedNode *prev;
    LinkedNode *next;
} LinkedList;
```

Advanced Programming Techniques

```
/* Creates and initializes a doubly-linked list. */
LinkedList *createList(void) {
    LinkedList *list = malloc(sizeof(*list));

    /* Fool the computer into thinking the dummy node
     * is a separate structure even though it is
     * actually stored as part of the list itself. */
    list->head = (LinkedNode *)&list->prev;

    /* Initialize the list to be empty by making the
     * first and last node pointers within the dummy
     * node point to the dummy node itself. */
    LinkedNode *head = list->head;
    head->prev = head->next = head;
    return list;
}


/* Frees all the nodes in this list. */
void freeList(LinkedList *list) {
    LinkedNode *head = list->head;
    LinkedNode *prev, *curr = head->next;
    while ((prev = curr) != head) {
        curr = curr->next;
        freeNode(prev);
    }
    list->head = NULL;
    free(list);
}


/* Returns true if this list is empty; otherwise returns false. */
int listIsEmpty(const LinkedList *list) {
    LinkedNode *head = list->head;
    return head->next == head;
}


/* Returns a pointer to the node in this list at
 * location index or NULL if no such node exists. */
LinkedNode *getNode(const LinkedList *list, int index) {
    LinkedNode *head = list->head;
    LinkedNode *curr = head->next;
    while (curr != head) {
        if (index == 0) {
            return curr;
        }
        --index;
        curr = curr->next;
    }
    return NULL;
}
```

```c
/* Returns a pointer to the node in this list that
 * contains key or NULL if no such node exists. */
LinkedNode *findNode(const LinkedList *list, int key) {
    LinkedNode *head = list->head;
    LinkedNode *curr = head->next;
    while (curr != head) {
        if (curr->which == key) {
            return curr;
        }
        curr = curr->next;
    }
    return NULL;
}


/* Inserts a node at the beginning of this list. */
void insertNode(LinkedList *list, LinkedNode *node) {
    LinkedNode *head = list->head;
    node->prev = head;
    node->next = head->next;
    head->next->prev = node;
    head->next = node;
}


/* Appends a node at the end of this list. */
void appendNode(LinkedList *list, LinkedNode *node) {
    LinkedNode *head = list->head;
    node->prev = head->prev;
    node->next = head;
    head->prev->next = node;
    head->prev = node;
}


/* Removes a node from this list. */
void removeNode(LinkedList *list, LinkedNode *node) {
    /* Ensure node is actually in this list. */
    if (findNode(list, node->which) != NULL) {
        node->prev->next = node->next;
        node->next->prev = node->prev;
        node->prev = node->next = NULL;
    }
}
```

Linked List Comparison

The following table compares the four different styles of linked lists presented in this chapter. The speed measurement in the table is for a test program that repeatedly calls insertNode, appendNode, and removeNode. The complexity column shows the *cyclomatic complexity* for four functions from each of the linked lists.

Comparison of Linked List Data Structures

Example	Name	Relative Speed (1 is best)	Dummy Nodes	Complexity	
1	Node centric, singly-linked list	1.08	0	insertNode	2
				appendNode	2
				removeFirst	3
				removeNode	5
				total	**12**
2	Node centric, singly-linked list with a dummy node	1.00	1	insertNode	2
				appendNode	1
				removeFirst	2
				removeNode	4
				total	**9**
3	Pointer centric, singly-linked list	1.00	0	insertNode	2
				appendNode	1
				removeFirst	2
				removeNode	4
				total	**9**
7	Doubly-linked list	1.11	1	insertNode	1
				appendNode	1
				removeFirst	2
				removeNode	2
				total	**6**

From the table, we see that the pointer centric singly-linked list is only slightly faster than the node centric singly-linked list and the doubly-linked list, so the performance difference is probably insignificant in most programs. However, the reduced complexity of the pointer centric, singly-linked list is a sufficient reason to switch from the node centric to the pointer centric. It is also interesting to see that the complexity of the doubly-linked list is even lower than the pointer centric singly-linked list. If you are not worried about the extra memory required for a doubly-linked list, it may be the best choice.

Programming Exercises

1. Read about the cyclomatic complexity metric and count the complexity of the `freeList` and `findNode` functions as written in the node centric singly-linked list code.
2. Use the pointer centric singly-linked list code in this chapter to help you write a singly-linked list that uses a string (`const char *`) as the key for each node instead of an integer.

4

Iteration and Recursion

Iteration

Iteration is the process of repeating a block of statements in a computer program by using a repetition control structure, also known as a loop. Here is a simple example of iteration written in Java that computes *n* factorial (*n!*).

Example 1

```
/** Iteratively computes n factorial (n!)
 * which is n * (n-1) * (n-2) * ... 1 */
public static long factorial(int n) {
    long fact = n;
    while (--n > 1) {
        fact *= n;
    }
    return fact;
}
```

Desk Check

n	fact
4	

Recursion

Recursion is the process of repeating a block of statements in a computer program by using a recursive function. A *recursive function* is a function that calls itself either directly or indirectly. A function *F* calls itself indirectly by calling function *G* which calls function *F*. A recursive algorithm solves a problem by repeatedly dividing it into smaller sub-problems until reaching the simplest sub-problem and then solves that simplest problem. All recursive algorithms must have three parts:

1. A base case which is the simplest sub-problem and when the recursion will stop
2. Code to work toward the base case by dividing the problem into sub-problems
3. One or more recursive function calls

Parts 2 and 3 are often combined into a single line of code. As a student, the first example of a recursive function that I saw was one that computed *n* factorial as shown in example 2.

Example 2

```
/** Recursively computes n factorial (n!)
 * which is n * (n-1) * (n-2) * ... 1 */
public static long factorial(int n) {
    if (n == 1) {
        return 1;
    }
    return n * factorial(n - 1);
}
```

Function	Variables	
factorial	n	return
	4	
factorial	n	return
	.	
factorial	n	return
factorial	n	return

Notice in example 2 the three parts of a recursive algorithm. The base case is when $n == 1$, and the solution to 1 factorial is simply 1. Working toward the base case is done by splitting n factorial into $n * (n-1$ factorial). Working toward the base case and the recursive call to the factorial function are combined into one line of code. Figure 20 shows the order in which the recursive factorial function calls itself and returns from those calls.

As a student the recursive factorial example made no sense to me because I realized that n factorial could be easily computed using iteration as shown in example 1. Recursion began to make sense to me when I learned that

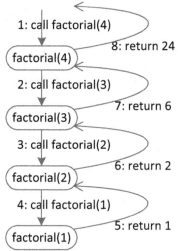

1: call factorial(4)

factorial(4)   8: return 24

2: call factorial(3)

factorial(3)   7: return 6

3: call factorial(2)

factorial(2)   6: return 2

4: call factorial(1)

factorial(1)   5: return 1

Figure 20: Function calls and returns for the recursive factorial function.

1. Recursion comes to computer science from mathematics, and mathematicians define some mathematical functions, such as the Fibonacci series, in a recursive form.
2. Some programming languages, such as Erlang, ProLog, and Haskell, don't include iteration because the inventors of those languages believed that iteration was error prone and that recursive solutions revealed the intrinsic structure of a problem.
3. There are many programming problems more complex than the simple recursive examples shown in text books, such as n factorial, that are elegantly solved using recursion.

Advantages of Recursion

Recursion has several advantages over iteration, including

1. If a computing problem can be broken into smaller self-similar problems, a recursive solution is almost always shorter and more elegant than an iterative solution.
2. A recursive function uses existing, well-understood, and tested functionality, namely the system stack, as part of its solution instead of requiring that another stack module be written.
3. It is sometimes necessary to prove that a computing solution is correct. Proving correctness is easier for a recursive solution than an iterative solution because recursion and proof by induction are closely related.

Disadvantages of Recursion

The disadvantages of recursion include the following.

1. Using recursion means many function calls. In many programming languages, a fuction call is relatively slow compared to other operations. In languages that don't include iteration, the language compiler or interpreter will transform some recursive functions into iterative ones to lower the number of function calls. If a programmer writes a recursive function in a language that doesn't include this optimization, that function will likely be much slower than an iterative function that solves the same problem.
2. Recursion can be hard to learn and understand especially for someone that has already learned iteration.
3. A recursive function may use all the memory in the system stack which will cause the program to crash. Try this simple Java program.

Example 3

```java
public class Crash {
    public static void main(String[] args) {
        fillTheStack(1);
    }

    /** Recursively calls itself until the system call stack
     * fills and the program crashes with a StackOverflowError.*/
    public static void fillTheStack(int frameNumber) {
        System.out.println(frameNumber);
        System.out.flush();
        fillTheStack(frameNumber + 1);
    }
}
```

How many numbers did the program print on your computer before filling the stack and crashing? My computer produced 11415, and then the program crashed. Of course, if the function fillTheStack declared local variables besides its one parameter, each function call would require a larger stack frame, and the program would produce fewer numbers before crashing.

Tail Recursion

Tail recursion is a special form of recursion where a recursive function calls itself as its final action. Here is an iterative function to compute the greatest common divisor (gcd) of two integers and the same functionality written as a tail recursive function.

Example 4

```java
/** Iteratively computes the greatest
 * common divisor of two integers. */
public static long gcd(long x, long y) {
    // Loop until the greatest common divisor is found.
    long rem;   // Holds the remainder
    do {
        rem = x % y;
        x = y;
        y = rem;
    } while (rem != 0);
    return x;
}
```

Desk Check

x	y	rem
472	24	

Example 5

```java
/** Recursively computes the greatest
 * common divisor of two integers. */
public static long gcd(long x, long y) {
    long rem = x % y;
    if (rem == 0) {
        return y;
    }
    return gcd(y, rem);
}
```

Desk Check

Function	Variables			
gcd	x	y	rem	return
	472	24		
gcd	x	y	rem	return
gcd	x	y	rem	return

Figure 21 shows the order in which the recursive gcd function calls itself and returns from those calls. Many programming languages automatically convert a tail call to a goto statement or an assembly language JUMP instruction which makes a tail recursive function execute as quickly as an iterative function. From Figure 21 it is easy to see why a compiler can optimize a tail recursive call into a JUMP instruction. Notice that every return shown in Figure 21 returns the same value, which is the value returned by the last call to the gcd function.

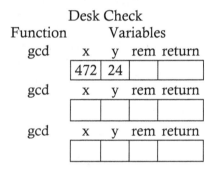
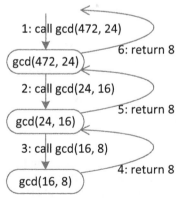

Figure 21: Function calls and returns for the recursive gcd function.

Converting Recursion to Iteration

Programming languages without recursion and with only iteration for repeating statements have been proven to be *Turing complete*. The same is true for programming languages that have no iterative control structures and use only recursion for repetition. This means that both types of languages can solve the same types of computing problems. Or in other words, any recursive solution can be converted to an iterative solution and vice versa.

Some programming languages don't include recursion. Also, some companies, notably defense companies, don't allow their software developers to use recursion because of the possibility of a recursive function overflowing the call stack. Imagine if one of the programs in an F-35 fighter jet overflowed its call stack and crashed while the plane was flying. This might cause the plane to launch its weapons prematurely or cause the plane to crash. Programmers working in these environments must convert recursive functions to iterative ones.

All tail recursive functions can be converted into iterative functions that use a simple loop and vice versa. Many recursive functions that are not tail recursive can be converted to tail recursive functions by adding accumulator parameters. All other recursive functions can be converted to iterative functions by writing and using a stack in place of the system call stack.

Tail Recursion to Iteration

All tail recursive functions can be converted into iterative functions that use a simple loop and vice versa. Consider this simple tail recursive function that prints integers backwards from *n* down to 1.

Example 6

```
/** Recursively prints the numbers backwards from n down to 1. */
public static void countDown(int n) {
    if (n > 0) {
        System.out.println(n);
        countDown(n - 1);
    }
}
```

Notice how easily it is converted to an iterative function with a simple loop.

Example 7

```
/** Iteratively prints the numbers backwards from n down to 1. */
public static void countDown(int n) {
    for (;  n > 0;  n--) {
        System.out.println(n);
    }
}
```

Non-Tail Recursion to Tail Recursion

Any tail recursive function can be converted to an iterative function and vice versa. So what can a programmer do with a non-tail recursive function? First convert it to a tail recursive function then convert that to an iterative function. Here is a non-tail recursive function that computes the sum of the numbers in an array. It is not tail recursive because the call from the sumR function to itself is not the last action in the sumR function. After the call returns, the last action is addition.

Example 8

```
public static double sum(double[] a) {
    return sumR(a, 0);
}

/** Recursively computes the sum of the numbers in a. */
private static double sumR(double[] a, int i) {
    if (i == a.length) {
        return 0;
    }
    return a[i] + sumR(a, i + 1);
}
```

Desk Check

Function	Variables			return
sum	a			
	6.5	7.1	6.9	
	[0]	[1]	[2]	

This non-tail recursive function can be converted to a tail recursive function by adding an accumulator parameter (the parameter s in the sumR function below) and moving the addition into the arguments of the recursive call to sumR.

Function		i	return
sumR			
sumR		i	return
sumR		i	return
sumR		i	return

Example 9

```
public static double sum(double[] a)
{
    return sumR(0, a, 0);
}

/** Recursively computes the sum of the numbers in a. */
private static double sumR(double s, double[] a, int i) {
    if (i == a.length) {
        return s;
    }
    return sumR(s + a[i], a, i+1);
}
```

Desk Check

Function	Variables			return
sum	a			
	6.5	7.1	6.9	
	[0]	[1]	[2]	
sumR		s	i	return
sumR		s	i	return
sumR		s	i	return
sumR		s	i	return

This tail recursive function is easily converted to iteration.

Example 10

```
/** Iteratively computes the sum of the numbers in a. */
public static double sum(double[] a) {
    double sum = 0;
    for (int i = 0;  i < a.length;  ++i) {
        sum += a[i];
    }
    return sum;
}
```

The recursive factorial function listed at the beginning of this chapter is another example of a non-tail recursive function that is easily converted to tail recursion by adding a helper function and an accumulator parameter and moving the multiplication into the arguments to the recursive call.

Example 11

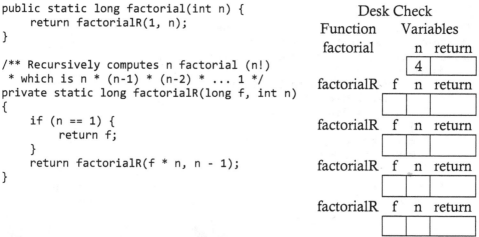

```
public static long factorial(int n) {
    return factorialR(1, n);
}

/** Recursively computes n factorial (n!)
 * which is n * (n-1) * (n-2) * ... 1 */
private static long factorialR(long f, int n)
{
    if (n == 1) {
        return f;
    }
    return factorialR(f * n, n - 1);
}
```

Desk Check

Function	Variables		
factorial		n	return
		4	
factorialR	f	n	return
factorialR	f	n	return
factorialR	f	n	return
factorialR	f	n	return

Converting Other Recursion to Iteration

Some non-tail recursive functions, including recursive functions that call themselves from multiple locations, cannot be converted to tail recursion. The straight forward way, although not always the best way, to convert such a recursive function to an iterative one, is for a programmer to create and use his own stack in place of the system call stack. Then the code in the iterative function must simulate calling and returning from the function by pushing and popping variables on the stack.

Binary Tree

Consider a binary search tree that stores a string at each node as shown in the UML class diagram in Figure 22. Figure 23 shows an instance of this binary search tree that has a name stored at each node. Any function that traverses the entire tree can be written as a recursive or iterative function. Here is a recursive Java function that traverses the tree and returns the length of the longest string that is stored within the tree.

Node
–left : Node
–right : Node
–data : String
+Node(data : String)

BinTree
–root : Node
+BinTree()
+add(data : String) : void
+maxLen() : int
+toList() : ArrayList<String>

Figure 22: A UML class diagram for a binary search tree.

Example 12

```java
/** Returns the length of the
 * longest String stored in
 * this binary tree. */
public int maxLen() {
    return maxLenR(root, 0);
}
```

```java
/** Recursively finds the length of the longest
 * String stored in this binary tree. */
private static int maxLenR(Node curr, int max) {
    if (curr != null) {
        int len = curr.data.length();
        if (len > max) {
            max = len;
        }
        max = maxLenR(curr.left, max);
        max = maxLenR(curr.right, max);
    }
    return max;
}
```

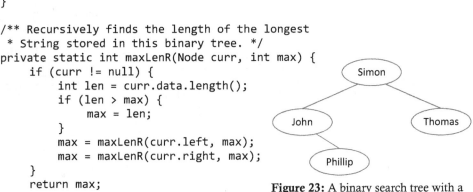

Figure 23: A binary search tree with a name stored at each node.

Desk Check

Function Variables
maxLen return

| | |
| --- | |

maxLenR curr max len

maxLenR curr max len   curr max len

maxLenR curr max len   curr max len   curr max len   curr max len

maxLenR   curr max len   curr max len

Here is an iterative Java function that also returns the length of the longest string stored within a binary tree. Notice that this iterative function maintains its own stack as it traverses the tree which makes the iterative solution more complex than the recursive one.

Example 13

```java
/* The Java API documentation suggests that programmers should
 * use ArrayDeque for a stack, but we can't use ArrayDeque here
 * because it throws a NullPointerException when we push NULL
 * on the stack, so we have to write our own stack class. */
private static final class Stack<E> extends ArrayList<E> {
    void push(E e) { add(e); }
    E pop() { return remove(size() - 1); }
}


/** Iteratively finds the length of the
 * longest String stored in this binary tree. */
public int maxLen() {
    int max = 0;
    Stack<Node> stack = new Stack<Node>();
    stack.push(root);
    while (stack.size() > 0) {
        Node curr = stack.pop();
        if (curr != null) {
            int len = curr.data.length();
            if (len > max) {
                max = len;
            }
            stack.push(curr.right);
            stack.push(curr.left);
        }
    }
    return max;
}
```

Desk Check

stack

[0]   [1]   [2]

curr len max

The recursive maxLenR function performs a pre-order traversal of a binary tree. Here is a recursive function that performs an in-order traversal of a binary search tree and produces an array list containing all the data in the binary search tree in sorted order.

Example 14

```java
/** Returns an array list that contains all the data in this tree. */
public ArrayList<String> toList() {
    ArrayList<String> list = new ArrayList<String>();
    toListR(list, root);
    return list;
}

/** Recursively builds an array list that
 * contains all the data in this binary tree. */
private static void toListR(ArrayList<String> list, Node curr) {
    if (curr != null) {
        toListR(list, curr.left);
        list.add(curr.data);
        toListR(list, curr.right);
    }
}
```

A pre-order traversal is easier to convert to iteration than an in-order traversal because the pre-order requires each node to be pushed and popped from the stack only once and the in-order requires each node to be pushed and popped twice. Additionally, an in-order traversal requires a return pointer or task flag to be pushed on the stack. During an in-order traversal this task flag determines if the action to be performed on the current node is to check its left node or to process its data. Here is an iterative function converted from the previous recursive function that performs an in-order traversal of a binary search tree. Notice how each node is pushed on the stack twice, once with a flag of CheckLeft and once with a flag of Process.

Desk Check

Function	Variables				
toList	list				
toListR	curr				
toListR	curr			curr	
toListR	curr	curr		curr	curr
toListR		curr	curr		

Example 15

```java
private static enum ToDo { CheckLeft, Process };

private static final class Frame {
    Node node;
    ToDo todo;
    Frame(Node n, ToDo t) { node = n;  todo = t; }
}
```

Advanced Programming Techniques

```
private static final class Stack<E> extends ArrayList<E> {
    void push(E e) { add(e); }
    E pop() { return remove(size() - 1); }
}

/** Iteratively builds an array list of the data in this binary tree. */
public ArrayList<String> toList() {
    ArrayList<String> list = new ArrayList<String>();
    if (root != null) {
        Stack<Frame> stack = new Stack<Frame>();
        stack.push(new Frame(root, ToDo.CheckLeft));
        while (stack.size() > 0) {
            Frame frame = stack.pop();
            Node curr = frame.node;
            switch (frame.todo) {
            case CheckLeft:
                frame.todo = ToDo.Process;
                stack.push(frame);
                if (curr.left != null) {
                    stack.push(new Frame(curr.left, ToDo.CheckLeft));
                }
                break;
            case Process:
                list.add(curr.data);
                if (curr.right != null) {
                    /* We no longer need the frame for the current
                     * node, so reuse it for the right child. */
                    frame.node = curr.right;
                    frame.todo = ToDo.CheckLeft;
                    stack.push(frame);
                }
                break;
            }
        }
    }
    return list;
}
```

Desk Check

list

stack

frame

node	todo

Fibonacci Series

Consider the Fibonacci series that starts with 0 and 1: 0, 1, 1, 2, 3, 5, 8... which mathematicians define as a recursive function:

$$fib(n) = fib(n-2) + fib(n-1)$$
$$fib(1) = 1$$
$$fib(0) = 0$$

Here is a recursive Java function to compute the nth Fibonacci number. Notice that this recursive function is essentially a direct translation of the mathematical function into Java.

Example 16

```java
/** Recursively computes the nth Fibonacci number. */
public static long fibonacci(int n) {
    switch (n) {
        case 0:   return 0;
        case 1:   return 1;
        default:  return fibonacci(n-2) + fibonacci(n-1);
    }
}
```

Desk Check

Function Variables
fibonacci n   return

| 4 | |

fibonacci n   return   n   return

fibonacci n   return   n   return   n   return   n   return

fibonacci   n   return   n   return

Figure 24 shows the order in which the recursive fibonacci function calls itself and returns from those calls.

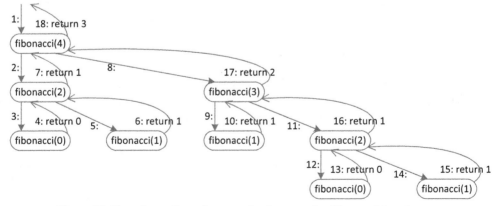

Figure 24: Function calls and returns for the recursive fibonacci function.

Here is an iterative Java function that computes the nth Fibonacci number by maintaining its own stack. This is a very complex way to compute Fibonacci numbers.

Example 17

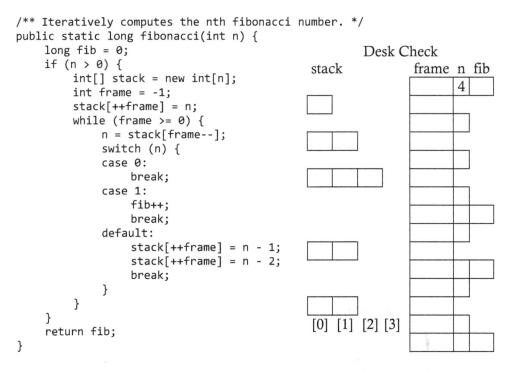

```java
/** Iteratively computes the nth fibonacci number. */
public static long fibonacci(int n) {
    long fib = 0;
    if (n > 0) {
        int[] stack = new int[n];
        int frame = -1;
        stack[++frame] = n;
        while (frame >= 0) {
            n = stack[frame--];
            switch (n) {
            case 0:
                break;
            case 1:
                fib++;
                break;
            default:
                stack[++frame] = n - 1;
                stack[++frame] = n - 2;
                break;
            }
        }
    }
    return fib;
}
```

Desk Check
stack   frame n fib
                       4
[0] [1] [2] [3]

Of course there is a shorter and faster iterative solution that doesn't maintain its own stack for computing the nth Fibonacci number. This shorter solution uses the fact that any Fibonacci number is simply the sum of the previous two Fibonacci numbers. So this solution simply adds two numbers repeatedly until it has computed the nth Fibonacci number.

Example 18

```java
/** Iteratively computes the nth Fibonacci number. */
public static long fibonacci(int n) {
    long past = 0;
    long present = 1;
    while (n > 0) {
        long future = past + present;
        past = present;
        present = future;
        --n;
    }
    return past;
}
```

Desk Check
future past present n
                       4

We can also convert the iterative `fibonacci` function in the previous example into a tail recursive function. This tail recursive function is much more efficient than the original recursive `fibonacci` function in example 16 because it adds the previous two Fibonacci numbers to produce the next number instead of repeatedly adding 0 and 1 as example 16 does.

Example 19

```java
public static long fibonacci(int n) {
    return fibonacciR(0, 1, n);
}

/** Recursively computes the nth Fibonacci number. */
private static long fibonacciR(long past, long present, int n) {
    if (n == 0) {
        return past;
    }
    return fibonacciR(present, past + present, n - 1);
}
```

Interestingly there is even a formula for computing the nth Fibonacci number.

$$fib(n) = \frac{\varphi^n - (-\varphi)^{-n}}{\sqrt{5}}$$

where φ is the *golden ratio*

$$\varphi = \frac{1 + \sqrt{5}}{2} \approx 1.618$$

Desk Check

Function fibonacci	n	return
	4	

fibonacciR	past	present	n	return

fibonacciR	past	present	n	return

fibonacciR	past	present	n	return

fibonacciR	past	present	n	return

fibonacciR	past	present	n	return

Example 20

```java
private static final double SQRT5 = Math.sqrt(5);
private static final double GOLDEN = (1 + SQRT5) / 2;

/** Computes the nth Fibonacci number. */
public static long fibonacci(int n) {
    double numer = Math.pow(GOLDEN, n) - Math.pow(-GOLDEN, -n);
    return Math.round(numer / SQRT5);
}
```

Desk Check

SQRT5	GOLDEN	n	numer	return
2.236	1.618	4		

Files and Directories

One common use of recursion is to process all the files in a file system directory and its sub directories. Below is a recursive function that builds a list of all files and sub directories in a directory. The list is sorted so that the files appear first in alphabetical order and the sub directories and their files appear second also in alphabetical order like this:

volunteer
volunteer\flora.jpg
volunteer\soccer
volunteer\soccer\improvements.rtf
volunteer\soccer\U6
volunteer\soccer\U6\rules.docx
volunteer\soccer\U6\Schedule.xlsx

Example 21

```java
/** Returns a list of all files and sub directories
 * in a directory and its sub directories. */
public static ArrayList<File> listFiles(File[] dir) {
    ArrayList<File> list = new ArrayList<File>();
    listFilesR(list, dir);
    return list;
}

/** Recursively lists the files in a directory. */
private static void listFilesR(ArrayList<File> list, File[] dir) {
    /* Sort the directory so that files are listed
     * in alphabetical order first, then directories
     * are listed in alphabetical order second. */
    Arrays.sort(dir, fileComp);
    int i = 0;

    // Add all non directory files to the list.
    for (; i < dir.length; ++i) {
        File file = dir[i];
        if (file.isDirectory()) {
            break;
        }
        list.add(file);
    }

    // Process all directories.
    for (; i < dir.length; ++i) {
        // Add this directory to the list of files.
        File file = dir[i];
        list.add(file);
        File[] subdir = file.listFiles();
        if (subdir != null) {
            // Recurse to process the files in this directory.
            listFilesR(list, subdir);
        }
    }
}
```

```
/** A Comparator to sort files and sub directories.
 * Files are listed first in alphabetical order, and
 * sub directories are listed second in alphabetical order. */
private static final FileComparator fileComp = new FileComparator();

private static class FileComparator implements Comparator<File> {
    @Override
    public int compare(File f1, File f2) {
        boolean f1IsDir = f1.isDirectory();
        boolean f2IsDir = f2.isDirectory();
        int ret;
        if (f1IsDir == f2IsDir) {
            String n1 = f1.getName().toLowerCase();
            String n2 = f2.getName().toLowerCase();
            ret = n1.compareTo(n2);
        }
        else {
            ret = f1IsDir ? 1 : -1;
        }
        return ret;
    }
}
```

Of course this recursive function can be converted to an iterative one by creating
and maintaining a stack. In the following example, the stack holds only directories,
and the files and directories are added to a list just as in the previous example.

Example 22

```
/** Returns a list of all files and sub directories
 * in a directory and its sub directories. */
public static ArrayList<File> listFiles(File[] dir) {
    // A list of files and directories.
    ArrayList<File> list = new ArrayList<File>();

    // A stack of directories.
    Stack<File> stack = new Stack<File>();

    RevDirComparator revComp = new RevDirComparator();
    Arrays.sort(dir, revComp);
    addAndPush(list, stack, dir);

    while (!stack.isEmpty()) {
        // Add this directory to the list of files.
        File subdir = stack.pop();
        list.add(subdir);

        // Process the files in this directory.
        dir = subdir.listFiles();
        if (dir != null) {
            Arrays.sort(dir, revComp);
            addAndPush(list, stack, dir);
        }
    }
    return list;
}
```

Advanced Programming Techniques

```java
/** Adds all non directory files to list
 * and pushes all directories on stack. */
private static void addAndPush(
        ArrayList<File> list, Stack<File> stack, File[] dir) {
    int i = 0;

    // Add all non directory files to the list.
    for (;  i < dir.length;  ++i) {
        File file = dir[i];
        if (file.isDirectory()) {
            break;
        }
        list.add(file);
    }

    // Push all directories on the stack.
    for (;  i < dir.length;  ++i) {
        File file = dir[i];
        stack.push(file);
    }
}


/** A Comparator to sort files and sub directories.  Files are listed
 * first in alphabetical order.  Sub directories are listed second in
 * reverse alphabetical order because sub directories will be pushed
 * on and then popped off a stack. */
private static final class RevDirComparator implements Comparator<File>
{
    @Override
    public int compare(File f1, File f2) {
        boolean f1IsDir = f1.isDirectory();
        boolean f2IsDir = f2.isDirectory();
        int ret;
        if (f1IsDir == f2IsDir) {
            String n1 = f1.getName().toLowerCase();
            String n2 = f2.getName().toLowerCase();
            ret = n1.compareTo(n2);
            if (f1IsDir) {
                ret = -ret;  // Reverse the order of sub directories.
            }
        }
        else {
            ret = f1IsDir ? 1 : -1;
        }
        return ret;
    }
}
```

Converting Iteration to Recursion

To convert an iterative function to a recursive one, a programmer must divide a problem into smaller self-similar problems. Consider an iterative binary search function.

Example 23

```
/** If key is in list, returns any index where key is
 * located within list; otherwise returns -insertPoint - 1.
 * Assumes list is already sorted. */
public static int binarySearch(float[] list, float key) {
    int left = 0;
    int right = list.length - 1;
    while (left <= right) {
        int mid = left + ((right - left) >>> 1);
        float cmp = key - list[mid];
        if (cmp > 0) {
            left = mid + 1;
        } else if (cmp < 0) {
            right = mid - 1;
        } else {
            return mid;
        }
    }

    // key is not present in list, but if it
    // were, it would be stored at location left.
    return -(left + 1);
}
```

Desk Check

list

−2.1	−1	3.9	6.2	7.1	9.7	10	12	13.1	15.6	18	19	20.1	24.5
[0]	[1]	[2]	[3]	[4]	[5]	[6]	[7]	[8]	[9]	[10]	[11]	[12]	[13]

key	left	right	mid	cmp	return
15.6					

An iterative binary search function can be converted into a recursive function by realizing that a binary search repeatedly divides a list into halves and restricts the search to one of those halves. This leads to a simple recursive implementation. Notice within the binarySearchR function that each time it calls itself, it is dividing the search interval in half.

Example 24

```
/** If key is in list, returns any index where key is
 * located within list; otherwise returns -insertPoint - 1.
 * Assumes list is already sorted. */
public static int binarySearch(float[] list, float key) {
    return binarySearchR(list, key, 0, list.length - 1);
}

/** Recursively searches an array for any occurence of key. */
private static int binarySearchR(
        float[] list, float key, int left, int right) {
    if (left <= right) {
        int mid = left + ((right - left) >>> 1);
        float cmp = key - list[mid];
        if (cmp > 0) {
            return binarySearchR(list, mid + 1, right, key);
        } else if (cmp < 0) {
            return binarySearchR(list, left, mid - 1, key);
        } else {
            return mid;
        }
    }

    // key is not present in list, but if it
    // were, it would be stored at location left.
    return -(left + 1);
}
```

Desk Check

list

-2.1	-1	3.9	6.2	7.1	9.7	10	12	13.1	15.6	18	19	20.1	24.5
[0]	[1]	[2]	[3]	[4]	[5]	[6]	[7]	[8]	[9]	[10]	[11]	[12]	[13]

Function	Variables				
binarySearch	key	return				
	15.6					
binarySearchR	key	left	right	mid	cmp	return
	15.6					
binarySearchR	key	left	right	mid	cmp	return
	15.6					
binarySearchR	key	left	right	mid	cmp	return
	15.6					
binarySearchR	key	left	right	mid	cmp	return
	15.6					

Future Value

The future value of an investment with a constant growth rate can be calculated using this formula: $f = a\,(1 + r)^n$ where f is the future value, a is the investment amount (also known as the principal), r is the growth rate per period, and n is the total number of periods throughout the life of the investment. Here is a function that uses this formula to compute the future value.

Example 25

```
/** Computes the future value of an investment with
 * compound growth and a fixed annual growth rate. */
public static long futureValue(long principal,
        double annualRate, int years, int periodsPerYear) {
    double rate = annualRate / periodsPerYear;
    int periods = years * periodsPerYear;
    double fv = principal * Math.pow(1 + rate, periods);
    return (long)Math.rint(fv);
}
```

Desk Check

principal	annualRate	years	periodsPerYear	rate	periods	fv
10000	0.06	2	4			

The formula for computing the future value is derived using calculus and accounts for compound growth or interest. The future value can also be computed using iteration where the simple interest for one investment period is computed and added to the investment principal during each iteration.

Example 26

```
/** Iteratively computes the future value of an investment
 * with compound growth and a fixed annual growth rate. */
public static long futureValue(long principal,
        double annualRate, int years, int periodsPerYear) {
    double rate = annualRate / periodsPerYear;
    int periods = years * periodsPerYear;
    for (int i = 1;  i <= periods;  i++) {
        principal += (long)Math.rint(principal * rate);
    }
    return principal;
}
```

Desk Check

i	principal	annualRate	years	periodsPerYear	rate	periods
	10000	0.06	2	4		

Of course this iterative function can be converted to a tail recursive function that during each function call computes the simple interest for one investment period and adds that interest to the principal.

Example 27

```
public static long futureValue(long principal,
        double annualRate, int years, int periodsPerYear) {
    double rate = annualRate / periodsPerYear;
    int periods = years * periodsPerYear;
    return futureValueR(principal, rate, periods);
}

/** Recursively computes the future value of an investment
 * with compound growth and a fixed annual growth rate. */
private static long futureValueR(
        long principal, double rate, int period) {
    if (--period < 0) {
        return principal;
    }
    principal += (long)Math.rint(principal * rate);
    return futureValueR(principal, rate, period);
}
```

Desk Check

Function	Variables						
futureValue	principal	annualRate	years	periodsPerYear	rate	periods	return
	10000	0.06	2	4			
futureValueR	principal	rate	period	return			
futureValueR	principal	rate	period	return			
futureValueR	principal	rate	period	return			
futureValueR	principal	rate	period	return			
futureValueR	principal	rate	period	return			
futureValueR	principal	rate	period	return			
futureValueR	principal	rate	period	return			
futureValueR	principal	rate	period	return			
futureValueR	principal	rate	period	return			

Conclusions

Iteration and recursion are equally powerful tools for causing a computer to repeat a group of statements. All recursive functions can be rewritten as iterative functions which a programmer may need to do if she is writing a program in a language that lacks recursion or that does not optimize recursion. All iterative functions can be rewritten as recursive functions which a programmer may need to do if he is writing a program in a language that lacks iteration.

5
Counting Bits

A *boolean variable*, named after the British mathematician George Boole, is a variable that holds either false or true and nothing else. Sometimes within a program we have many boolean variables, perhaps hundreds or thousands. An efficient way to store many boolean variables is in a group called a *bitset* where each boolean variable is stored in a single bit with 0 meaning false and 1 meaning true. If a bit within a bitset holds 0, we say it is *off* or *clear*, and if it holds 1, we say it is *on* or *set*.

One important operation that must be performed on a bitset is to count how many bits are set, which is sometimes called the *population count*. This chapter explores six different algorithms for computing the population count. Although counting bits is an important operation, it is unlikely you will ever be required to write code to do it. However, these six algorithms are highly instructive because they show very different approaches to the same problem, including straight forward or naive, combinatorial, and look-up.

Bitwise Operators

In order to understand the six population count algorithms, you must first understand the standard bitwise operations that a computer can perform: `left shift, unsigned right shift, signed right shift, not, and, or, exclusive or`. The following examples are written in Java, but most programming languages have similar bitwise operators.

Left Shift

The `left shift` operator is two less than symbols (`<<`) and shifts all the bits in an integer to the left by a specified number of locations, filling the rightmost bits with 0 and losing the values in the leftmost bits. Arithmetically this is the same as multiplying an integer by a power of two.

Example 1

```
int x = 53;
int pos = x << 2;   /* 53 * 4 = 212 */
int z = -42;
int neg = z << 2;   /* -42 * 4 = -168 */
```

Desk Check

	decimal	hexadecimal	binary
x	53	00000035	0000 0000 0000 0000 0000 0000 0011 0101
pos	212	000000d4	0000 0000 0000 0000 0000 0000 1101 0100
z	−42	ffffffd6	1111 1111 1111 1111 1111 1111 1101 0110
neg	−168	ffffff58	1111 1111 1111 1111 1111 1111 0101 1000

Unsigned Right Shift

The unsigned right shift operator (also called the logical right shift operator) is three greater than symbols (>>>) and shifts all the bits in an integer to the right by a specified number of locations, filling the leftmost bits with 0 and losing the values in the rightmost bits. Arithmetically this is the same as dividing any **non-negative** integer by a power of two.

Example 2

```
int x = 53;
int pos = x >>> 2;   /*  53 / 4 = 13 */
int z = -42;
int neg = z >>> 2;   /* -42 / 4 != 1,073,741,813 */
```

Desk Check

	decimal	hexadecimal	binary
x	53	00000035	0000 0000 0000 0000 0000 0000 0011 0101
pos	13	0000000d	0000 0000 0000 0000 0000 0000 0000 1101
z	−42	ffffffd6	1111 1111 1111 1111 1111 1111 1101 0110
neg	1073741813	3ffffff5	0011 1111 1111 1111 1111 1111 1111 0101

Signed Right Shift

In a two's complement integer, the leftmost bit is the sign bit and contains a 0 if the integer is non-negative and contains a 1 if the integer is negative. The signed right shift operator (also called the arithmetic right shift operator) is two greater than symbols (>>) and shifts all the bits in an integer to the right by a specified number of locations, filling the leftmost bits with the value in the sign bit and losing the values in the rightmost bits. Arithmetically this is the same as dividing any **non-negative** integer by a power of two.

Example 3

```
int x = 53;
int pos = x >> 2;   /* 53 / 4 = 13 */
```

Desk Check

	decimal	hexadecimal	binary
x	53	00000035	0000 0000 0000 0000 0000 0000 0011 0101
pos	13	0000000d	0000 0000 0000 0000 0000 0000 0000 1101

Because signed right shift preserves the value of the sign bit, it is also the same as dividing any **negative** integer by a power of two **if** no 1 bits are lost when shifting right. In other words if you use signed right shift to divide negative integers by 2 (x >> 1), the answer will be the same as integer division only half the time. If you use signed right shift to divide negative integers by 4 (x >> 2), the answer will be the same as integer division only one fourth of the time, and so on.

Example 4

```
int w = -40;
int ssrw = w >> 2;   /* -40 / 4 == -10 */
int x = -41;
int ssrx = x >> 2;   /* -41 / 4 != -11 */
int y = -42;
int ssry = y >> 2;   /* -42 / 4 != -11 */
int z = -43;
int ssrz = z >> 2;   /* -43 / 4 != -11 */
```

Desk Check

	decimal	hexadecimal	binary
w	−40	ffffffd8	1111 1111 1111 1111 1111 1111 1101 1000
ssrw	−10	fffffff6	1111 1111 1111 1111 1111 1111 1111 0110
x	−41	ffffffd7	1111 1111 1111 1111 1111 1111 1101 0111
ssrx	−11	fffffff5	1111 1111 1111 1111 1111 1111 1111 0101
y	−42	ffffffd6	1111 1111 1111 1111 1111 1111 1101 0110
ssry	−11	fffffff5	1111 1111 1111 1111 1111 1111 1111 0101
z	−43	ffffffd5	1111 1111 1111 1111 1111 1111 1101 0101
ssrz	−11	fffffff5	1111 1111 1111 1111 1111 1111 1111 0101

The best way to use right shift with all integers and to get the same result as division by a power of 2 is to add $2^k - 1$ to negative integers before using signed right shift, where k is the number of bits to shift right. The next example demonstrates signed right shift to divide a negative number by 4.

Example 5

```
int x = -43;
if (x < 0) {
    x += (1 << 2) - 1;   /* can be simplified to x += 3; */
}
int div = x >> 2;   /* -43 / 2 == -10 */
```

Desk Check

	decimal	hexadecimal	binary
x	−43	ffffffd5	1111 1111 1111 1111 1111 1111 1101 0101
x	−40	ffffffd8	1111 1111 1111 1111 1111 1111 1101 1000
div	−10	fffffff6	1111 1111 1111 1111 1111 1111 1111 0110

Not

The bitwise not operator is the tilde (~) and takes an integer as input and clears every set bit and sets every clear bit, or in other words, switches every 1 bit to 0 and every 0 bit to 1.

Example 6

```
int x = 53;
int result = ~x;
```

Desk Check

	decimal	hexadecimal	binary
x	53	00000035	0000 0000 0000 0000 0000 0000 0011 0101
result	−54	ffffffca	1111 1111 1111 1111 1111 1111 1100 1010

And

The bitwise and operator is the ampersand (&) and takes two integers as input and produces an integer with bits set where the bits were set in both inputs and clear everywhere else. This is the same operation as logical and but performed on each bit. Within a program, bitwise and is often used to test if a bit is set and to clear bits in a variable.

Example 7

```
int x =  53;
int y = 107;
int result = x & y;
```

Desk Check

	decimal	hexadecimal	binary
x	53	00000035	0000 0000 0000 0000 0000 0000 0011 0101
y	107	0000006b	0000 0000 0000 0000 0000 0000 0110 1011
result	33	00000021	0000 0000 0000 0000 0000 0000 0010 0001

Or

The bitwise or operator is the vertical bar (|) and takes two integers as input and produces an integer with bits set where the bits were set in either or both inputs and clear everywhere else. This is the same operation as logical or but performed on each bit. Within a program, bitwise or is often used to set bits in a variable.

Example 8

```
int x =  53;
int y = 107;
int result = x | y;
```

Desk Check

	decimal	hexadecimal	binary
x	53	00000035	0000 0000 0000 0000 0000 0000 0011 0101
y	107	0000006b	0000 0000 0000 0000 0000 0000 0110 1011
result	127	0000007f	0000 0000 0000 0000 0000 0000 0111 1111

Exclusive Or

The bitwise exclusive or operator is the caret (^) and takes two integers as input and produces an integer with bits set where the bits in the two inputs were different and clear everywhere else. This is the same operation as logical exclusive or but performed on each bit. Within a program, bitwise exclusive or is often used in data encryption and can even be used to swap the values of two variables.

Example 9

```
int x =  53;
int y = 107;
int result = x ^ y;
```

Desk Check

	decimal	hexadecimal	binary
x	53	00000035	0000 0000 0000 0000 0000 0000 0011 0101
y	107	0000006b	0000 0000 0000 0000 0000 0000 0110 1011
result	94	0000005e	0000 0000 0000 0000 0000 0000 0101 1110

Shortcut Operators

All the bitwise operators, except not (~), can be combined with the assignment operator (=) to make shortcut operators as shown in the following examples.

Example 10

```
int x = 53;
x &= 0x0f;
x |= 0x70;
x ^= 0x6b;
x <<= 2;
x >>>= 1;
x >>= 1;
```

Desk Check

	decimal	hexadecimal	binary
int x = 53;			
x &= 0x0f;			
x |= 0x70;			
x ^= 0x6b;			
x <<= 2;			
x >>>= 1;			
x >>= 1;			

Example 11: Set and Clear Bits

```
int x = 53;
x |= (1 << 3);  // Turn on bit #3
// Test if bit #3 is turned on
if ((x & (1 << 3)) != 0) {
    System.out.println("bit 3 is set");
}
else {
    System.out.println("bit 3 is clear");
}
x &= ~(1 << 3);  // Turn off bit #3
```

Desk Check

	decimal	hexadecimal	binary
int x = 53;			
1 << 3			
x |= (1<<3);			
x & (1<<3)			
~(1 << 3)			
x &= ~(1<<3);			

Example 12: Encrypt and Decrypt a Short Message

```
long plain = 0x0000737570657262L;  // ASCII values for "superb"
long key = 0x36a1804be2f359e1L;
long cipher = plain ^ key;    // encrypt
long message = cipher ^ key;  // decrypt
```

Desk Check

	hexadecimal	binary
plain		
key		
cipher		
message		

Example 13: Switch the Values in Two Variables

```
int x = 53;
int y = -42;
x ^= y;  // Switch the values in x and y.
y ^= x;
x ^= y;
```

Desk Check

	decimal	hexadecimal	binary
int x = 53;			
int y = -42;			
x ^= y;			
y ^= x;			
x ^= y;			

Advanced Programming Techniques

Naive Bit Counting

A few years ago employees from a prominent software company would ask candidates during a job interview to write code to count the number of bits set to 1 in a 64-bit number. This is sometimes called the *population count*. Many candidates would write code similar to this naive Java code.

Example 14

```java
/** Returns the number of bits set in a 64-bit word. */
public static int nbits(long word) {
    int n = 0;
    for (int i = 0;  i != 64;  ++i) {
        if ((word & 1) != 0) {
            ++n;
        }
        word >>>= 1;
    }
    return n;
}
```

Desk Check

word	word & 1	n	i
0011 0101			

Improved Loop Termination

The interviewer would then show the candidate a faster way to solve the problem which was similar to this example.

Example 15

```java
/** Returns the number of bits set in a 64-bit word. */
public static int nbits(long word) {
    int n = 0;
    while (word != 0) {
        if ((word & 1) != 0) {
            ++n;
        }
        word >>>= 1;
    }
    return n;
}
```

Desk Check

word	word & 1	n
0011 0101		

Example 15 should be faster than example 14 because it eliminates incrementing the variable i, and it stops executing the loop when word reaches zero, meaning example 15 may not have to check all 64 bits. For example, consider this 64-bit word: 0x00 00 00 04 a0 3f 6e 8c. Example 15 will check only 35 bits and then stop, but example 14 will check all 64 bits before it finishes. Of course if a word has the highest order bit set, as is the case half of the time with random data, then example 15 isn't much faster. So, example 15 is slightly faster than example 14 but only very slightly. There are several other algorithms for computing the population count which are substantially faster.

Addition Instead of If

Computers often execute `if` statements slowly because modern CPUs have a pipeline of instructions that are in the process of being decoded and executed. When the CPU begins executing an `if-else` statement, before it knows the value of the condition (true or false), it will predict that value (usually as true) and begin speculatively executing the statements in the corresponding part of the `if-else` statement. However, when the CPU finishes calculating the value of the condition, if it has predicted incorrectly, it must unload the instruction pipeline and begin executing the statements in the other part of the `if-else` statement which takes time. When an `if` statement does not have a matching `else`, the CPU must still predict whether the condition is true or false and speculatively execute statements according to its prediction. So to avoid the performance penalty of an `if` statement, example 16 replaces the `if` statement with a statement that adds 0 or 1. On my computer example 16 executes in about one third the time of example 15.

Example 16

```
/** Returns the number of bits set in a 64-bit word. */
public static int nbits(long word) {
    int n = 0;
    while (word != 0) {
        n += (int)word & 1;
        word >>>= 1;
    }
    return n;
}
```

Desk Check

word	word & 1	n
0011 0101		

Skip Zero Bits

This next example takes advantage of a feature of two's complement arithmetic, namely: for any integer x, `x &= (x - 1)` deletes the rightmost set bit in x. This means example 17 simply skips the 0 bits. For random values of `word` about half the bits will be 0, so example 17 is about twice as fast as example 16 for random data.

Example 17

```
/** Returns the number of bits set in a 64-bit word. */
public static int nbits(long word) {
    int n = 0;
    while (word != 0) {
        ++n;
        word &= word - 1;
    }
    return n;
}
```

Desk Check

word	n	word - 1
0011 0101		

Combinatorial Algorithm

Example 18 is based on algorithm 1.3, page 3 of "Combinatorial Algorithms, Theory and Practice", by Edward M. Reingold, Jurg Nievergelt, and Narsingh Deo. This code is an example of a combinatorial algorithm or one that repeatedly combines intermediate results to arrive at the answer. Notice how this code repeatedly

1. shifts an integer to the right and uses a mask to extract every other bit (or every two bits or every four bits, etc),
2. uses the same mask to extract the other bits in the word, and
3. adds the bits, thus repeatedly combining intermediate results.

In essence, the code in example 18 uses a 64-bit processor as 32 2-bit processors, then 16 4-bit processors, then 8 8-bit processors, then 4 16-bit processors, 2 32-bits processors, and finally 1 64-bit processor to arrive at the answer. It runs in almost one fifth of the time of example 17.

Example 18

```
/** Returns the number of bits set in a 64-bit word. */
public static int nbits(long word) {
    final long
        ones  = 0x5555555555555555L,
        twos  = 0x3333333333333333L,
        fours = 0x0f0f0f0f0f0f0f0fL;
    word = (word >>>  1 & ones) + (word & ones);
    word = (word >>>  2 & twos) + (word & twos);
    word = ((word >>>  4) + word) & fours;
    word = (word >>>  8) + word;
    word = (word >>> 16) + word;
    word = (word >>> 32) + word;
    return (int)word & 0xff;
}
```

Desk Check

word	word >>> 1	ones	word >>> 1 & ones	word & ones
0011 0101				

	word >>> 2	twos	word >>> 2 & twos	word & twos

	word >>> 4		(word >>> 4) + word	fours

Look Up Table

Finally example 19 separates a 64-bit word into 8 bytes and uses a look-up table to determine how many bits are set in each byte and adds those 8 quantities together. This example runs approximately as fast as example 18 but requires 256 bytes of memory for storing the look-up table.

Example 19

```
/** The number of bits set in a byte. */
private static final byte onbits[] = {
    0, 1, 1, 2, 1, 2, 2, 3, 1, 2, 2, 3, 2, 3, 3, 4,
    1, 2, 2, 3, 2, 3, 3, 4, 2, 3, 3, 4, 3, 4, 4, 5,
    1, 2, 2, 3, 2, 3, 3, 4, 2, 3, 3, 4, 3, 4, 4, 5,
    2, 3, 3, 4, 3, 4, 4, 5, 3, 4, 4, 5, 4, 5, 5, 6,
    1, 2, 2, 3, 2, 3, 3, 4, 2, 3, 3, 4, 3, 4, 4, 5,
    2, 3, 3, 4, 3, 4, 4, 5, 3, 4, 4, 5, 4, 5, 5, 6,
    2, 3, 3, 4, 3, 4, 4, 5, 3, 4, 4, 5, 4, 5, 5, 6,
    3, 4, 4, 5, 4, 5, 5, 6, 4, 5, 5, 6, 5, 6, 6, 7,
    1, 2, 2, 3, 2, 3, 3, 4, 2, 3, 3, 4, 3, 4, 4, 5,
    2, 3, 3, 4, 3, 4, 4, 5, 3, 4, 4, 5, 4, 5, 5, 6,
    2, 3, 3, 4, 3, 4, 4, 5, 3, 4, 4, 5, 4, 5, 5, 6,
    3, 4, 4, 5, 4, 5, 5, 6, 4, 5, 5, 6, 5, 6, 6, 7,
    2, 3, 3, 4, 3, 4, 4, 5, 3, 4, 4, 5, 4, 5, 5, 6,
    3, 4, 4, 5, 4, 5, 5, 6, 4, 5, 5, 6, 5, 6, 6, 7,
    3, 4, 4, 5, 4, 5, 5, 6, 4, 5, 5, 6, 5, 6, 6, 7,
    4, 5, 5, 6, 5, 6, 6, 7, 5, 6, 6, 7, 6, 7, 7, 8
};

/** Returns the number of bits set in a 64-bit word. */
public static int nbits(long word) {
    return onbits[(int)(word >>> 56)] +
        onbits[(int)(word >>> 48) & 0xff] +
        onbits[(int)(word >>> 40) & 0xff] +
        onbits[(int)(word >>> 32) & 0xff] +
        onbits[(int)(word >>> 24) & 0xff] +
        onbits[(int)(word >>> 16) & 0xff] +
        onbits[(int)(word >>>  8) & 0xff] +
        onbits[(int) word & 0xff];
}
```

Desk Check

word	(int)word & 0xff	onbits[(int)word & 0xff]
0011 0101		

Algorithm Comparison

The following table compares all six of the algorithms presented in this chapter. Notice that the combinatorial and look up algorithms are **21 times** faster than the naive algorithm. From the table, it is clear that example 18, the combinatorial algorithm, is the best overall choice of algorithms to count how many bits are set to 1 within an integer. Within the Java 1.6 libraries, the method `Long.bitCount` uses a slightly modified version of example 18.

Comparison of Bit Counting Algorithms on 64-bit Random Data

Example	Name	Relative Speed (1 is best)	Speed Depends on the Input	Data Storage (bytes)
14	Naive	21	no	0
15	Improved Loop Termination	21	yes	0
16	Addition Instead of If	9	yes	0
17	Skip Zero Bits	5	yes	0
18	Combinatorial	1	no	24
19	Look up	1	no	256

6
Sets

Many computer programming problems deal with sets. In naive set theory, a *set* is simply a collection of unique elements; in other words, none of the elements are repeated in the set. A *list* is also a collection of elements, but a list may contain duplicate elements. People often use the term list for something that is really a set. For example, the list of employees at a company is really a set because each employee's information appears only once in the list. The same is true for the list of students in a class or the list of cars on a sales lot. All of these are really sets and not just lists.

There are multiple operations that we want a computer to perform with sets, such as

- contains - determine if some element is a member of a set
- is subset - determine if a set is a subset of another set
- equals - determine if a set is equal to another set
- intersect - compute the intersection of two sets
- union - compute the union of two sets
- relative complement - compute the complement of one set within another set

Because this list of operations is so long and because the operations are all related, a set should be designed and implemented in a program as a class.

One difficulty with computing set operations is that the size of the resultant set is not known until after computing the set operation. This means the computer does not know how much memory to allocate for storing the result set until after computing the contents of the result set. There are at least three solutions to this problem.

1. Compute the result twice: the first time counting the size of the result set, and the second time storing the results.
2. Before computing the result, determine a maximum bound to the size of the result set. Allocate an array with this maximum size. Compute and store the result in the array. Truncate the array to the actual size of the result set if necessary.
3. Compute the set operation storing the result in a collection that can grow such as a Java `ArrayList` or a Visual Basic Collection.

The first two Java classes in this chapter, `StringSet` and `SortedStringSet`, use solution 2. The last class, `StringBitSet`, uses solution 3.

Unsorted Sets

Figure 25 shows a UML class diagram for class StringSet. An object created from this class stores a set of Strings in an array and does not assume the Strings are sorted. The code for this class is below and uses naive or obvious algorithms based on the linear search algorithm. These naive algorithms are simple and quickly implemented but will execute slowly for large sets.

StringSet
–array : String[]
+StringSet(a : String[]) –StringSet(n : int) +size() : int +contains(term : String) : boolean +isSubset(setB : StringSet) : boolean +equals(setB : StringSet) : boolean +intersect(setB : StringSet) : StringSet +relCompl(setB : StringSet) : StringSet +union(setB : StringSet) : StringSet

Figure 25: A UML class diagram for an unsorted set of strings.

```java
import java.util.Arrays;

/** An unsorted set of Strings. */
public class StringSet {
    /** The array that holds the elements of this set. */
    private final String[] array;

    /** Creates a StringSet from an array. */
    public StringSet(String[] a) {
        array = Arrays.copyOf(a, a.length);
    }

    /** Creates a StringSet from an array but using
     * only the first n elements of that array. */
    private StringSet(String[] a, int n) {
        array = Arrays.copyOfRange(a, 0, n);
    }

    /** Returns the number of elements in this set. */
    public int size() { return array.length; }
```

Example 1: Determine If an Element Is a Member of a Set

```java
    /** Returns true if this set contains the
     * specified term; otherwise returns false. */
    public boolean contains(String term) {
        for (int i = 0;  i < array.length;  ++i) {
            if (array[i].equals(term)) {
                return true;
            }
        }
        return false;
    }
```

Desk Check

array

"apple"	"pear"	"plum"	"cherry"	"peach"
[0]	[1]	[2]	[3]	[4]

term	i	return

Example 2: Determine If a Set Is a Subset

```
/** Returns true if this set is a subset
 * of setB; otherwise returns false. */
public boolean isSubset(StringSet setB) {
    for (int i = 0;  i < this.array.length;  ++i) {
        String termA = this.array[i];
        if (!setB.contains(termA)) {
            return false;
        }
    }
    return true;
}
```

Desk Check

this: `"elm"` `"pine"` `"rose"`
        [0]   [1]   [2]

setB: `"lilac"` `"pine"` `"fir"` `"elm"`
         [0]   [1]   [2]   [3]

i	termA	return

```
/** Returns true if this set is equal
 * to setB; otherwise returns false. */
public boolean equals(StringSet setB) {
    return this.size() == setB.size() && this.isSubset(setB);
}
```

Example 3: Compute the Intersection of Two Sets

```
/** Returns the intersection of this set and setB. */
public StringSet intersect(StringSet setB) {
    // Allocate an array large enough to hold the results.
    int ceil = Math.min(this.size(), setB.size());
    String[] arrayC = new String[ceil];

    // Compute the intersection of this set and setB.
    int n = 0;
    for (int i = 0;  i < this.array.length;  ++i) {
        String termA = this.array[i];
        if (setB.contains(termA)) {
            arrayC[n++] = termA;
        }
    }

    // Return a new set that contains the results.
    return new StringSet(arrayC, n);
}
```

Desk Check

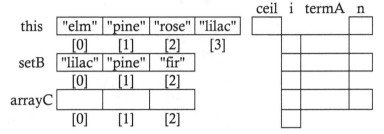

					ceil	i	termA	n
this	"elm"	"pine"	"rose"	"lilac"				
	[0]	[1]	[2]	[3]				
setB	"lilac"	"pine"	"fir"					
	[0]	[1]	[2]					
arrayC								
	[0]	[1]	[2]					

Example 4: Compute the Complement of a Set Relative to Another

```
/** Returns the complement of setB within this set. */
public StringSet relCompl(StringSet setB) {
    // Allocate an array large enough to hold the results.
    int ceil = this.size();
    String[] arrayC = new String[ceil];

    // Compute the complement of setB within this set.
    int n = 0;
    for (int i = 0;  i < this.array.length;  ++i) {
        String termA = this.array[i];
        if (!setB.contains(termA)) {
            arrayC[n++] = termA;
        }
    }

    // Return a new set that contains the results.
    return new StringSet(arrayC, n);
}
```

Desk Check

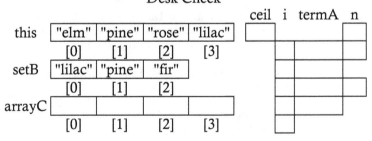

					ceil	i	termA	n
this	"elm"	"pine"	"rose"	"lilac"				
	[0]	[1]	[2]	[3]				
setB	"lilac"	"pine"	"fir"					
	[0]	[1]	[2]					
arrayC								
	[0]	[1]	[2]	[3]				

Example 5: Compute the Union of Two Sets

```java
/** Returns the union of this set and setB. */
public StringSet union(StringSet setB) {
    // Allocate an array large enough to hold the results.
    int ceil = this.size() + setB.size();
    String[] arrayC = new String[ceil];

    // Compute the union of this set and setB by
    // 1. copying to setC all the elements in this set, and
    for (int i = 0;  i < this.array.length;  ++i) {
        arrayC[i] = this.array[i];
    }
    int n = this.array.length;

    // 2. copying to setC all the elements that
    // appear in setB but not in this set.
    for (int i = 0;  i < setB.array.length;  ++i) {
        String termB = setB.array[i];
        if (!this.contains(termB)) {
            arrayC[n++] = termB;
        }
    }

    // Return a new set that contains the results.
    return new StringSet(arrayC, n);
}
```

Desk Check

this	"elm"	"pine"	"rose"	"lilac"
	[0]	[1]	[2]	[3]

setB	"lilac"	"pine"	"fir"
	[0]	[1]	[2]

arrayC	"elm"	"pine"	"rose"	"lilac"	"fir"		
	[0]	[1]	[2]	[3]	[4]	[5]	[6]

ceil i termB n

```java
/** Returns a string representation of this set. */
@Override
public String toString() {
    return Arrays.toString(array);
}
}
```

Sorted Sets

If the elements in our sets are sorted, we can use much faster algorithms when computing set operations. If a set is sorted, we can use the binary search algorithm to determine if an element is a member of that set. Also, if two sets are sorted, we can use merge algorithms to determine if one set is a subset of the other and to compute the intersection, union, and other set operations.

A *merge algorithm* computes a set operation by simultaneously iterating through two or more sorted sets and merging the sets together. This merging is far faster than the naive algorithms shown previously in this chapter because the naive algorithms read through the data in set B multiple times, but the merge algorithms read through both sets only once. In fact, if two sets, A and B, contain m and n elements, respectively, the naive intersection algorithm will perform a maximum of $m * n$ comparisons, but the merge intersection algorithm will perform a maximum of $m + n - 1$ comparisons. As m and n become large, this makes a huge difference in the number of comparisons needed to compute the intersection as shown in Figure 26.

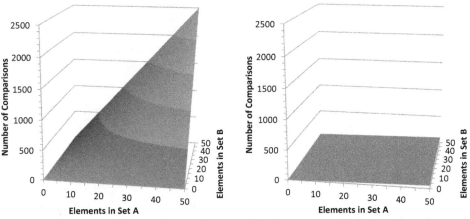

Figure 26: Maximum number of comparisons required to compute the intersection of two sets using a naive algorithm versus using a merge algorithm.

Figure 27 shows a UML class diagram for a sorted set class. An object made from this class holds one set of strings, always keeps that set in sorted order, and uses merge algorithms to compute the intersection, relative complement, and union of two sets as shown in the Java code below.

SortedStringSet
−array : String[]
+SortedStringSet(a : String[]) −SortedStringSet(n : int) +size() : int +contains(term : String) : boolean +isSubset(setB : SortedStringSet) : boolean +equals(setB : SortedStringSet) : boolean +intersect(setB : SortedStringSet) : SortedStringSet +relCompl(setB : SortedStringSet) : SortedStringSet +union(setB : SortedStringSet) : SortedStringSet

Figure 27: A UML class diagram for a sorted set of strings.

```java
import java.util.Arrays;

/** A sorted set of Strings. */
public class SortedStringSet {
    /** The array that holds the elements of this set. */
    private final String[] array;

    /** Creates a SortedStringSet from an array. */
    public SortedStringSet(String[] a) {
        // Create and sort a copy of the array a.
        array = Arrays.copyOf(a, a.length);
        Arrays.sort(array);
    }

    /** Creates a SortedStringSet from an array using
     * only the first n elements of that array. */
    private SortedStringSet(String[] a, int n) {
        array = Arrays.copyOfRange(a, 0, n);
    }

    /** Returns the number of elements in this set. */
    public int size() { return array.length; }

    /** Returns true if this set contains the
     * specified term; otherwise returns false. */
    public boolean contains(String term) {
        return Arrays.binarySearch(array, term) >= 0;
    }
}
```

Example 6: Determine If a Set Is a Subset

```java
/** Returns true if this set is a subset
 * of setB; otherwise returns false. */
public boolean isSubset(SortedStringSet setB) {
    int sizeA = this.size();
    int sizeB = setB.size();
    int a = 0, b = 0;
    while (a < sizeA && b < sizeB) {
        int cmp = this.array[a].compareTo(setB.array[b]);
        if (cmp < 0) {
            return false;
        } else if (cmp == 0) {
            a++;
        }
        b++;
    }
    return a == sizeA;
}
```

Desk Check

sizeA	sizeB	a	b	cmp	return

this

"elm"	"pine"	"rose"
[0]	[1]	[2]

setB

"elm"	"fir"	"lilac"	"pine"
[0]	[1]	[2]	[3]

```java
/** Returns true if this set is equal
 * to setB; otherwise returns false. */
public boolean equals(SortedStringSet setB) {
    return this.size() == setB.size() && this.isSubset(setB);
}
```

Example 7: Compute the Intersection of Two Sets

```java
/** Returns the intersection of this set and setB. */
public SortedStringSet intersect(SortedStringSet setB) {
    // Allocate an array large enough to hold the results.
    int sizeA = this.size();
    int sizeB = setB.size();
    int ceil = Math.min(sizeA, sizeB);
    String[] arrayC = new String[ceil];

    // Copy the elements that are in both this set
    // and setB to setC using a merge algorithm.
    // Assumes both sets are sorted.
    int a = 0, b = 0, n = 0;
    while (a < sizeA && b < sizeB) {
        String termA = this.array[a];
        String termB = setB.array[b];
        int cmp = termA.compareTo(termB);
        if (cmp < 0) {
            a++;
        } else if (cmp > 0) {
            b++;
        } else {
            arrayC[n++] = termA;
            a++;
            b++;
        }
    }

    // Return a new set that contains the results.
    return new SortedStringSet(arrayC, n);
}
```

Desk Check

	a	termA	b	termB	cmp	n

this: | "elm" [0] | "lilac" [1] | "pine" [2] | "rose" [3] |

setB: | "fir" [0] | "lilac" [1] | "pine" [2] |

arrayC: | [0] | [1] | [2] |

sizeA	sizeB	ceil

Example 8: Compute the Complement of a Set Relative to Another

```java
/** Returns the complement of setB within this set. */
public SortedStringSet relCompl(SortedStringSet setB) {
    // Allocate an array large enough to hold the results.
    int sizeA = this.size();
    int sizeB = setB.size();
    int ceil = sizeA;
    String[] arrayC = new String[ceil];

    // Copy the elements that are in setA (this) but
    // not in setB to setC using a merge algorithm.
    // Assumes both sets are sorted.
    int a = 0, b = 0, n = 0;
    while (a < sizeA && b < sizeB) {
        int cmp = this.array[a].compareTo(setB.array[b]);
        if (cmp < 0) {
            arrayC[n++] = this.array[a++];
        } else if (cmp > 0) {
            b++;
        } else {
            a++;
            b++;
        }
    }
    while (a < sizeA) {
        arrayC[n++] = this.array[a++];
    }

    // Return a new set that contains the results.
    return new SortedStringSet(arrayC, n);
}
```

Desk Check

						a	termA	b	termB	cmp	n
this	"elm"	"lilac"	"pine"	"rose"							
	[0]	[1]	[2]	[3]							
setB	"fir"	"lilac"	"pine"								
	[0]	[1]	[2]								
arrayC											
	[0]	[1]	[2]	[3]				sizeA	sizeB	ceil	

Example 9: Compute the Union of Two Sets

```java
/** Returns the union of this set and setB. */
public SortedStringSet union(SortedStringSet setB) {
    // Allocate an array large enough to hold the results.
    int sizeA = this.size();
    int sizeB = setB.size();
    int ceil = sizeA + sizeB;
    String[] arrayC = new String[ceil];

    // Copy the elements that are in setA (this) or
    // in setB to setC using a merge algorithm.
    // Assumes both sets are sorted.
    int a = 0, b = 0, n = 0;
    while (a < sizeA && b < sizeB) {
        int cmp = this.array[a].compareTo(setB.array[b]);
        if (cmp < 0) {
            arrayC[n++] = this.array[a++];
        } else if (cmp > 0) {
            arrayC[n++] = setB.array[b++];
        } else {
            arrayC[n++] = this.array[a++];
            b++;
        }
    }
    while (a < sizeA) {
        arrayC[n++] = this.array[a++];
    }
    while (b < sizeB) {
        arrayC[n++] = setB.array[b++];
    }

    // Return a new set that contains the results.
    return new SortedStringSet(arrayC, n);
}
```

Desk Check

	a	termA	b	termB	cmp	n

this: "elm"[0] "lilac"[1] "pine"[2] "rose"[3]

setB: "fir"[0] "lilac"[1] "pine"[2]

sizeA sizeB ceil

arrayC: "elm"[0] "fir"[1] "lilac"[2] "pine"[3] "rose"[4] [5] [6]

```java
/** Returns a string representation of this set. */
@Override
public String toString() {
    return Arrays.toString(array);
}
}
```

Bit Sets

Another way to store sets is to store all possible elements in a single large set, which in set theory a mathematician would call the *universe*. Then each set can be represented as a bitset. (See chapter 5 for the definition of a bitset.) If an element from the universe is not present in a set, then its corresponding bit in the bitset is 0. If an element is present in a set, then its corresponding bit in the bitset is 1.

Representing sets as bitsets may save memory depending on how large the universe is and how large each set is. Also, storing sets as bitsets dramatically speeds up the set operations because no comparisons are needed to compute the intersection, complement, or union of sets. Instead of comparisons, the set operations are computed using the bitwise operators: `not`, `and`, `or`, `exclusive or`. Notice in the code below how simple the functions `isSubset`, `intersect`, `relCompl`, and `union` are.

StringBitSet
−universe : Universe
−bitset : BitSet
+StringBitSet(a : String[])
−StringBitSet(original : StringBitSet)
+add(term : String) : void
+remove(term : String) : void
+size() : int
+contains(term : String) : boolean
+isSubset(setB : StringBitSet) : boolean
+equals(setB : StringBitSet) : boolean
+intersect(setB : StringBitSet) : StringBitSet
+relCompl(setB : StringBitSet) : StringBitSet
+union(setB : StringBitSet) : StringBitSet

Universe
−list : ArrayList<String>
−map : HashMap<String, Integer>
+Universe()
+size() : int
+get(index : int) : String
+find(term : String) : int
+add(term : String) : int

Figure 28: A UML class diagram for a set of strings implemented with a bitset.

```java
import java.util.ArrayList;
import java.util.BitSet;
import java.util.HashMap;

/** A set of Strings. */
public class StringBitSet {
    /** A shared list of all the terms stored in all sets. */
    private static final Universe universe = new Universe();

    /** The bitset that represents the terms in this set. */
    private final BitSet bitset;

    /** Creates a set from an array of Strings. */
    public StringBitSet(String[] a) {
        bitset = new BitSet(universe.list.size());
        for (String s : a) {
            add(s);
        }
    }
}
```

```
/** Creates a new set that is a copy of an existing set. */
public StringBitSet(StringBitSet original) {
    bitset = (BitSet)original.bitset.clone();
}

/** Returns the number of terms in this set. */
public int size() { return bitset.cardinality(); }
```

Example 10: Add an Element to a Set

```
/** Adds the specified term to this set if it is not
 * already present.  Returns true if the set was changed. */
public boolean add(String term) {
    boolean found;
    int index = universe.find(term);
    if (index == -1) {
        found = false;
        index = universe.add(term);
        bitset.set(index);
    }
    else {
        found = bitset.get(index);
        if (!found) {
            bitset.set(index);
        }
    }
    return !found;
}
```

Desk Check

universe.list

"elm"	"pine"	"rose"	"lilac"				
[0]	[1]	[2]	[3]	[4]	[5]	[6]	[7]

bitset	term	index	found	i	return
0101 0000	"fir"				

Example 11: Remove an Element from a Set

```
/** Removes the specified term from this set if it
 * is present.  Returns true if the set was changed. */
public boolean remove(String term) {
    boolean found = false;
    int index = universe.find(term);
    if (index != -1) {
        found = bitset.get(index);
        bitset.clear(index);
    }
    return found;
}
```

Desk Check

universe.list

"elm"	"pine"	"rose"	"lilac"	"fir"	"ash"		
[0]	[1]	[2]	[3]	[4]	[5]	[6]	[7]

bitset	term	index	i	found	return
1101 1000	"pine"				

Example 12: Determine if an Element Is a Member of a Set

```
/** Returns true if this set contains the
 * specified term; otherwise returns false. */
public boolean contains(String term) {
    boolean found = false;
    int index = universe.find(term);
    if (index != -1) {
        found = bitset.get(index);
    }
    return found;
}
```

Desk Check

universe.list

"elm"	"pine"	"rose"	"lilac"	"fir"	"ash"		
[0]	[1]	[2]	[3]	[4]	[5]	[6]	[7]

bitset	term	index	found
1101 1000	"lilac"		

Example 13: Determine if a Set is a Subset

```
/** Returns true if this set is a subset
 * of setB; otherwise returns false. */
public boolean isSubset(StringBitSet setB) {
    BitSet temp = (BitSet)this.bitset.clone();
    temp.and(setB.bitset);
    return temp.equals(this.bitset);
}
```

Desk Check

universe.list

"elm"	"pine"	"rose"	"lilac"	"fir"	"ash"		
[0]	[1]	[2]	[3]	[4]	[5]	[6]	[7]

this.bitset	setB.bitset	temp	return
1110 000	1101 1000		

```
/** Returns true if this set is equal
 * to setB; otherwise returns false. */
public boolean equals(StringBitSet setB) {
    return this.bitset.equals(setB.bitset);
}
```

Example 14: Compute the Intersection of Two Sets

```
/** Returns the intersection of this set and setB. */
public StringBitSet intersect(StringBitSet setB) {
    StringBitSet result = new StringBitSet(this);
    result.bitset.and(setB.bitset);
    return result;
}
```

Desk Check

universe.list

"elm"	"pine"	"rose"	"lilac"	"fir"	"ash"		
[0]	[1]	[2]	[3]	[4]	[5]	[6]	[7]

this.bitset   setB.bitset   result.bitset

1110 0000	1101 1000	

Example 15: Compute the Complement of a Set Relative to Another

```
/** Returns the complement of setB in this set. */
public StringBitSet relCompl(StringBitSet setB) {
    StringBitSet result = new StringBitSet(this);
    result.bitset.andNot(setB.bitset);
    return result;
}
```

Desk Check

universe.list

"elm"	"pine"	"rose"	"lilac"	"fir"	"ash"		
[0]	[1]	[2]	[3]	[4]	[5]	[6]	[7]

this.bitset   setB.bitset   result.bitset

1110 0000	1101 1000	

Example 16: Compute the Union of Two Sets

```
/** Returns the union of this set and setB. */
public StringBitSet union(StringBitSet setB) {
    StringBitSet result = new StringBitSet(this);
    result.bitset.or(setB.bitset);
    return result;
}
```

Desk Check

universe.list

"elm"	"pine"	"rose"	"lilac"	"fir"	"ash"		
[0]	[1]	[2]	[3]	[4]	[5]	[6]	[7]

this.bitset   setB.bitset   result.bitset

1110 0000	1101 1000	

Advanced Programming Techniques

```java
/** Returns a string representation of this set. */
@Override
public String toString() {
    StringBuilder sb = new StringBuilder();
    sb.append("[");
    String separator = "";
    for (int i = 0;  (i = bitset.nextSetBit(i)) != -1;  ++i) {
        sb.append(separator).append(universe.get(i));
        separator = ", ";
    }
    sb.append("]");
    return sb.toString();
}


/** The universe of all Strings that can appear in StringBitSets.*/
private static final class Universe {
    /** A list of all the terms in this universe. */
    private final ArrayList<String> list = new ArrayList<String>();

    /** A map from a term to its
     * corresponding index in this universe. */
    private final HashMap<String, Integer> map =
            new HashMap<String, Integer>();

    /** Returns the number of elements in this universe. */
    public int size() { return list.size(); }

    /** Returns the term in this universe located at index. */
    public String get(int index) { return list.get(index); }

    /** Returns the index of a term within  this universe if
     * it exists in this universe; otherwise returns -1. */
    public int find(String term) {
        Integer index = map.get(term);
        return index != null ? index.intValue() : -1;
    }

    /** Adds a term to this universe. */
    public int add(String term) {
        int i = list.size();
        list.add(term);
        map.put(term, new Integer(i));
        return i;
    }
}
}
```

7
Statistics

Statistical measurements are extremely useful in computer programs especially in clustering data. This chapter shows how to correctly compute common statistical values: minimum, median, maximum, sum, mean, variance, standard deviation, and correlation coefficient and shows how to translate mathematical summation expressions ($\sum$) into computer code.

Minimum

There are several ways to find the minimum value in a series of numbers. The algorithm shown below uses a loop that will cause the computer to compare every value in an array to a *running minimum*. At any point during the execution of the code, the running minimum holds the smallest value that the computer has encountered. When the computer reaches the end of the array, the running minimum will hold the actual minimum value of the series.

Example 1

```
/** Returns the minimum value stored in an array. */
public static double minimum(double[] data) {
    double min = data[0];
    for (int i = 1;  i < data.length;  ++i) {
        if (data[i] < min) {
            min = data[i];
        }
    }
    return min;
}
```

Desk Check

data				i	min
9	12.3	−3	5		
[0]	[1]	[2]	[3]		

To find the maximum value in an array, simply modify the above code to look for the largest value instead of the smallest value. In other words, modify the above code by changing the less than operator (<) to the greater than operator (>) and by changing the variable name min to max.

Another way to find the minimum and maximum values in an array is to sort the values in the array in ascending order. Then the minimum value will be stored in the first location of the array, and the maximum value will be stored in the last.

Summation

Often within a program, we have a series of numbers stored in an array, and the program needs to calculate the *sum* of those numbers. Summation is shown in mathematical notation using an upper case Greek sigma ($\sum$) like this.

$$\sum_{i=1}^{n} x_i$$

where X represents the entire series, x_i represents a single value within that series at location i, and n is the number of values within that series. The previous symbols can be read as "the sum of the series X from the 1st value to the nth value, inclusive." In other words:

$$\sum_{i=1}^{n} x_i = x_1 + x_2 + \cdots + x_n$$

When we write a program to compute the sum of a series of numbers stored in an array, we simply write a loop to add all the values in that array. This simple operation is also known as *accumulation* and is shown in the following examples.

Arrays in C, C++, Java, JavaScript, VB.NET, and many other languages are zero-based, meaning the very first element is always at location 0 within the array. Because of this, when writing code in these languages, we think of the mathematical summation expressions with i starting at zero like this:

$$\sum_{i=0}^{n-1} x_i$$

instead of the way shown above.

Example 2

```
/** Returns the sum of the values stored in an array. */
public static double sum(double[] data) {
    double s = 0;
    for (int i = 0;  i < data.length;  ++i) {
        s += data[i];
    }
    return s;
}
```

Desk Check

data				i	s
7	3	-2	4.4		
[0]	[1]	[2]	[3]		

Example 3 uses a for each loop to perform the same summation as example 2. Some programmers prefer the for each loop (example 3) over the standard counting loop (example 2) because it is shorter to write.

Example 3

```
/** Returns the sum of the values stored in an array. */
public static double sum(double[] data) {
    double s = 0;
    for (double x : data) {
        s += x;
    }
    return s;
}
```

Desk Check

data

7	3	-2	4.4
[0]	[1]	[2]	[3]

X   S

Mean

The statistical *mean* of a series of numbers is the expected or average value of that series. The mean is often represented by the Greek letter mu (μ) and is defined by this formula:

$$\mu = \frac{1}{n}\sum_{i=1}^{n} x_i = \frac{x_1 + x_2 + \cdots + x_n}{n}$$

where X represents a series with n values and x_i is a single value within that series at location i.

From this formula we see that the most obvious way to compute the mean of a series of numbers is to first compute the sum of that series and then divide the sum by the number of values in the series. The previous two code examples show how to compute the sum of a series, so example 4 calls one of the previous two examples.

Example 4

```
/** Returns the average of the values stored in an array. */
public static double mean(double[] data) {
    double s = sum(data);
    return s / data.length;
}
```

Desk Check

data

7	3	-2	4.4
[0]	[1]	[2]	[3]

s   return

Variance

The *variance* of a series of a numbers, which is represented by the Greek letter sigma squared, (σ^2) is a measure of how disperse or spread out the numbers are from the mean. A related measure is the *standard deviation* which is represented by the Greek letter sigma, (σ) and is simply the square root of the variance. The variance is defined by this formula.

$$\sigma^2 = \frac{1}{n}\sum_{i=1}^{n} (x_i - \mu)^2$$

From this formula the most obvious way to compute the variance is to first compute the mean (μ), which requires one pass through the data. Then compute the variance by subtracting the mean from each value in the series, squaring this difference and summing the squared values, all of which requires a second pass through the data. Here is the Java code to compute the variance with two passes through the data.

Example 5

```java
/** Computes the variance with two passes through the data. */
public static double varianceTwoPass(double[] data) {
    final double m = mean(data);   // First pass.
    double sqsum = 0.0;

    // Second pass.
    for (int i = 0;  i < data.length;  ++i) {
        double x = data[i];
        double t = x - m;
        sqsum += t * t;
    }
    double var = sqsum / data.length;
    return var;
}
```

Desk Check

data

7	3	-2	4.4
[0]	[1]	[2]	[3]

m	i	x	t	sqsum	var

With a little algebra we can rewrite the variance formula and see how to compute the variance with only one pass through the data. The formula for the variance is

$$\sigma^2 = \frac{1}{n}\sum_{i=1}^{n}(x_i - \mu)^2$$

By expanding (multiplying) the squared portion of the summation we get

$$\sigma^2 = \frac{1}{n}\sum_{i=1}^{n}(x_i^2 - 2\mu x_i + \mu^2)$$

Addition can be separated, so separating the parts of the summation gives us

$$\sigma^2 = \frac{1}{n}\sum_{i=1}^{n}x_i^2 - \frac{1}{n}\sum_{i=1}^{n}2\mu x_i + \frac{1}{n}\sum_{i=1}^{n}\mu^2$$

However, 2μ and μ^2 are both independent of the summation (they do not include any reference to i). So we can place the independent parts outside of the summations.

$$\sigma^2 = \frac{1}{n}\sum_{i=1}^{n}x_i^2 - 2\mu\frac{1}{n}\sum_{i=1}^{n}x_i + \mu^2\frac{1}{n}\sum_{i=1}^{n}1$$

Advanced Programming Techniques

Recall that the formula for the mean is

$$\mu = \frac{1}{n}\sum_{i=1}^{n} x_i$$

and that

$$\sum_{i=1}^{n} 1 = n$$

We can substitute both of these formulas into the formula for the variance.

$$\sigma^2 = \frac{1}{n}\sum_{i=1}^{n} x_i^2 - 2\mu\mu + \mu^2\frac{1}{n}n$$

which can be simplified as

$$\sigma^2 = \frac{1}{n}\sum_{i=1}^{n} x_i^2 - \mu^2$$

This final equation shows us how to compute the variance with only a single pass of the data. During that single pass of the data, we must compute two sums, (1) the sum of the numbers squared and (2) the sum of the numbers needed for the mean.

Example 6

```
/** Computes the variance with a
 * single pass through the data. */
public static double varianceOnePass(double[] data) {
    double sum = 0.0;
    double sqsum = 0.0;
    for (int i = 0;  i < data.length;  ++i) {
        double x = data[i];
        sum += x;
        sqsum += x * x;
    }
    double n = data.length;
    double mean = sum / n;
    double var = sqsum / n - mean * mean;
    return var;
}
```

Desk Check

data
7	3	-2	4.4
[0]	[1]	[2]	[3]

i	x	sum	sqsum	n	mean	var

Correlation

The *correlation coefficient* of two series of numbers or samples is a measure of the strength of a linear relationship between the two samples. The correlation coefficient is usually called just the *correlation* and is represented by the Greek letter rho (ρ) and is always a number in the range $[-1, 1]$. A correlation near -1 or 1

means the two samples are linearly related. A correlation near 0 means the two samples are not linearly related.

The formula for the correlation of two samples, X and Y, is:

$$\rho_{xy} = \frac{\sigma_{xy}}{\sigma_x \sigma_y}$$

where σ_{xy} is the covariance of the two samples and σ_x and σ_y are the standard deviations of X and Y respectively. The formula for the covariance of X and Y is

$$\sigma_{xy} = \frac{1}{n} \sum_{i=1}^{n} (x_i - \mu_x)(y_i - \mu_y)$$

We could use the previous formula for the correlation and this formula for the covariance to help us write a function to compute the correlation. However, this function would require two passes of each sample, X and Y, in order to compute the correlation.

We can rewrite these formulas using steps similar to those used in the section on variance which will enable us to write a function to compute the correlation with only a single pass of each sample. To rewrite the covariance formula, we first multiply the two parenthesized expressions which gives

$$\sigma_{xy} = \frac{1}{n} \sum_{i=1}^{n} (x_i y_i - \mu_x y_i - \mu_y x_i + \mu_x \mu_y)$$

Separating the summation into parts gives

$$\sigma_{xy} = \frac{1}{n} \sum_{i=1}^{n} x_i y_i - \frac{1}{n} \sum_{i=1}^{n} \mu_x y_i - \frac{1}{n} \sum_{i=1}^{n} \mu_y x_i + \frac{1}{n} \sum_{i=1}^{n} \mu_x \mu_y$$

Removing the terms that are independent of i from the summations yields

$$\sigma_{xy} = \frac{1}{n} \sum_{i=1}^{n} x_i y_i - \mu_x \frac{1}{n} \sum_{i=1}^{n} y_i - \mu_y \frac{1}{n} \sum_{i=1}^{n} x_i + \mu_x \mu_y \frac{1}{n} \sum_{i=1}^{n} 1$$

Substituting the definition for the means of X and Y and using

$$\sum_{i=1}^{n} 1 = n$$

gives

$$\sigma_{xy} = \frac{1}{n} \sum_{i=1}^{n} x_i y_i - \mu_x \mu_y - \mu_y \mu_x + \mu_x \mu_y \frac{1}{n} n$$

Simplifying, we get

$$\sigma_{xy} = \frac{1}{n} \sum_{i=1}^{n} x_i y_i - \mu_x \mu_y$$

Substituting this formula for covariance and the formulas for the standard deviation of X and Y into our original equation for correlation gives us

$$\rho_{xy} = \frac{\frac{1}{n} \sum_{i=1}^{n} x_i y_i - \mu_x \mu_y}{\sqrt{\frac{1}{n} \sum_{i=1}^{n} x_i^2 - \mu_x^2} \sqrt{\frac{1}{n} \sum_{i=1}^{n} y_i^2 - \mu_y^2}}$$

This final equation shows us how to compute the correlation with only a single pass through the two samples. During that single pass, the computer must compute the covariance of X and Y and the variance of X and the variance of Y, which requires the computer to compute five sums.

1. the sum of the X values
2. the sum of the X values squared
3. the sum of the Y values
4. the sum of the Y values squared
5. the sum of the product of the X and Y values

As you read the correlation code below you can see each of these summations.

Example 7

```
/** Computes the correlation coefficient of two samples. */
public static double correlation(double[] dataX, double[] dataY) {
    double sumX, sumY, sumX2, sumY2, sumXY;
    sumX = sumY = sumX2 = sumY2 = sumXY = 0.0;
    for (int i = 0;  i < dataX.length;  ++i) {
        double x = dataX[i];
        double y = dataY[i];
        sumX += x;
        sumY += y;
        sumX2 += x * x;
        sumY2 += y * y;
        sumXY += x * y;
    }
    double n = dataX.length;
    double meanX = sumX / n;
    double meanY = sumY / n;
    double sdevX = Math.sqrt(sumX2 / n - meanX * meanX);
    double sdevY = Math.sqrt(sumY2 / n - meanY * meanY);
    double covar = sumXY / n - meanX * meanY;
    double correl = covar / (sdevX * sdevY);
    return correl;
}
```

Desk Check

dataX

12	4	3.9	2.1
[0]	[1]	[2]	[3]

dataY

12	3.2	3.5	1.9
[0]	[1]	[2]	[3]

i	x	y	sumX	sumY	sumX2	sumY2	sumXY

n	meanX	meanY	sdevX	sdevY	covar	correl

Numerical Stability

Computers do not perform arithmetic in the same way that humans do. Humans use ideal arithmetic when adding, subtracting, multiplying, and dividing real numbers. Computers do not use ideal arithmetic but instead represent real numbers as IEEE 754 floating point numbers which are base 2 numbers with three parts, the *sign*, the *significand* (sometimes called the *fraction* or *mantissa*), and the *exponent*.

$$sign -4.7013267 \times 10^{26} \; exponent$$
$$significand$$

The significand and exponent are represented with a limited number of bits (binary digits) or in other words with limited precision. Because of this limited precision, a computer sometimes loses accuracy when performing arithmetic. For example, when I run a simple Java program that uses double precision floating point arithmetic to add $0.1 + 0.2$, my computer calculates a result of 0.30000000000000004 which is close but incorrect. Losing accuracy during a computation is called numerical instability, and if it is bad enough in an algorithm, the computer will simply give the wrong answer.

All the previous algorithms shown in this chapter are simple and easy to understand but are known to be numerically unstable for some data. For example the `mean` function shown earlier in this chapter returns `Infinity` as the average value of this series $[6.0\times10^{307}, 6.0\times10^{307}, 2.0\times10^{307}, 6.0\times10^{307}]$. However, examining the series, it is clear that the mean is really 5×10^{307}.

This section shows algorithms to compute the mean, variance, and correlation with improved numerical stability. To understand how these algorithms are derived, we will rewrite the function for computing the mean of a series of numbers. Here is the formula for computing the mean of a series of n values.

$$\mu = \frac{1}{n}\sum_{i=1}^{n} x_i = \frac{x_1 + x_2 + \cdots + x_{n-1} + x_n}{n}$$

We can rewrite the right hand side of the above equation by grouping the values $x_1 + x_2 + \ldots + x_{n-1}$ and then multiplying and dividing that group by $(n-1)$.

$$\mu = \frac{\frac{(n-1)(x_1 + x_2 + \cdots + x_{n-1})}{n-1} + x_n}{n}$$

Notice that

$$\frac{x_1 + x_2 + \cdots + x_{n-1}}{n-1}$$

is simply the mean of the first $n-1$ values in the series. So we can rewrite the equation for the mean of all n values as a recursive equation

$$\mu_n = \frac{(n-1)\mu_{n-1} + x_n}{n}$$

which is recursive because μ_n depends on μ_{n-1}. Distributing the $(n-1)$ gives this equation

$$\mu_n = \frac{n\mu_{n-1} - \mu_{n-1} + x_n}{n}$$

and simplifying results in

$$\mu_n = \mu_{n-1} + \frac{x_n - \mu_{n-1}}{n}$$

We can use this formula for μ_n to write the formula for μ_{n-1}.

$$\mu_{n-1} = \mu_{n-2} + \frac{x_{n-1} - \mu_{n-2}}{n-1}$$

We can substitute the formula for μ_{n-1} for the first occurrence of μ_{n-1} which gives

$$\mu_n = \mu_{n-2} + \frac{x_{n-1} - \mu_{n-2}}{n-1} + \frac{x_n - \mu_{n-1}}{n}$$

We can continue to substitute the recursive definitions for the first occurrence of each mean until we get

$$\mu_n = \mu_0 + \frac{x_1 - \mu_0}{1} + \frac{x_2 - \mu_1}{2} + \cdots + \frac{x_{n-1} - \mu_{n-2}}{n-1} + \frac{x_n - \mu_{n-1}}{n}$$

We can rewrite this equation using summation like this

$$\mu_n = \sum_{i=1}^{n} \frac{x_i - \mu_{i-1}}{i}$$

where $\mu_0 = 0$. From this equation we can see how to implement the mean function in a way that gives more stable results. This stable implementation is shown below. As you examine the code, recall that Java arrays are zero-based and that series in the equations above are one-based. This difference forces us to write i in the equations as $i+1$ in the code.

Example 8

```
/** Returns the average of the values stored in an array. */
public static double meanStable(double[] data) {
    /* Sort the data so that all small values such as 0.000000003
     * will be at the beginning of the array, and their contribution
     * to the mean of the data will not be lost because of the
     * precision of the CPU. */
    java.util.Arrays.sort(data);

    double mean = data[0];
    for (int i = 1;  i < data.length;  ++i) {
        double delta = data[i] - mean;
        mean += delta / (i + 1);
    }
    return mean;
}
```

Desk Check

data					i	delta	mean
-2	3	4.4	7				
[0]	[1]	[2]	[3]				

To understand how the above code works, it is helpful to see a graph of the data and delta and mean as shown in Figure 29. Notice how the mean is a *running mean*. The mean starts at the same value as the first data element, and then as each new element is processed, it holds the mean of all the previously processed elements. In other words, as each new data element is processed the mean moves closer and closer to the mean of all the data.

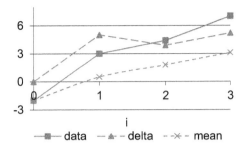

Figure 29: A graph of the data, delta, and mean values.

Just as we did for the mean, we can rewrite the formulas for computing the variance of a series and the correlation of two series to make computing the variance and correlation more stable. However, I will spare you the details of deriving these formulas. Here is Java code for computing the variance and the correlation in a numerically stable way.

Example 9

```java
/** Returns the variance of a series of numbers. */
public static double varianceStable(double[] data) {
    /* Sort the data so that all small values such as 0.000000003
     * will be at the beginning of the array and their contribution
     * to the variance of the data will not be lost because of the
     * precision of the CPU. */
    java.util.Arrays.sort(data);

    double mean = data[0];
    double sqsum = 0.0;
    for (int i = 1;  i < data.length;  ++i) {
        double weight = i / (i + 1.0);
        double delta = data[i] - mean;
        mean += delta / (i + 1);
        sqsum += delta * delta * weight;
    }
    double var = sqsum / data.length;
    return var;
}
```

Desk Check

data

-2	3	4.4	7
[0]	[1]	[2]	[3]

i	weight	delta	mean	sqsum	var

Example 10

```
/** Computes the correlation coefficient of two samples. */
public static double correlationStable(double[] dataX, double[] dataY) {
    double meanX = dataX[0];
    double meanY = dataY[0];
    double sumX2, sumY2, sumXY;
    sumX2 = sumY2 = sumXY = 0.0;
    for (int i = 1;  i < dataX.length;  ++i) {
        double weight = i / (i + 1.0);
        double deltaX = dataX[i] - meanX;
        double deltaY = dataY[i] - meanY;
        sumX2 += deltaX * deltaX * weight;
        sumY2 += deltaY * deltaY * weight;
        sumXY += deltaX * deltaY * weight;
        meanX += deltaX / (i + 1);
        meanY += deltaY / (i + 1);
    }
    double n = dataX.length;
    double sdevX = Math.sqrt(sumX2 / n);
    double sdevY = Math.sqrt(sumY2 / n);
    double covar = sumXY / n;
    double correl = covar / (sdevX * sdevY);
    return correl;
}
```

Multiple Statistics at Once

The minimum, median, maximum, count, sum, mean, variance, and standard deviation can all be computed with a sort and a single computation pass of the sorted data as shown in the Stats constructor below. Because this function is computing eight different values and because a Java function can return only one value, we need to define a class and create an object to hold the eight values. The class is shown in a UML class diagram in Figure 30.

Stats
−min : double
−med : double
−max : double
−sum : double
−mean : double
−var : double
−sdev : double
−count : int
+Stats(data : double[])   +toString() : String

Figure 30: A UML class diagram for a class to calculate multiple statistics at one time.

```
public class Stats {
    private double min, median, max;
    private double sum, mean, var, sdev;
    private int count;
```

Example 11

```java
public Stats(double[] data) {
    count = data.length;

    /* Sort the data so that all seemingly insignificant
     * values such as 0.000000003 will be at the beginning
     * of the array and their contribution to the mean and
     * variance of the data will not be lost because of
     * the precision of the CPU. */
    java.util.Arrays.sort(data);

    /* Since the data is now sorted, the minimum value
     * is at the beginning of the array, the median
     * value is in the middle of the array, and the
     * maximum value is at the end of the array. */
    min = data[0];
    int half = data.length / 2;
    median = data[half];
    if (isEven(data.length)) {
        median = (data[half - 1] + median) / 2.0;
    }
    max = data[data.length - 1];

    /* Compute the mean and variance using
     * a numerically stable algorithm. */
    double sqsum = 0.0;
    mean = data[0];
    for (int i = 1;  i < data.length;  ++i) {
        double x = data[i];
        double weight = i / (i + 1.0);
        double delta = x - mean;
        mean += delta / (i + 1.0);
        sqsum += delta * delta * weight;
    }

    sum = mean * count;
    var = sqsum / count;
    sdev = Math.sqrt(var);
}
```

Desk Check

data			
-2	3	4.4	7
[0]	[1]	[2]	[3]

i	x	weight	delta	mean	sqsum

count	min	med	max	sum	var	sdev

```
    public static boolean isEven(int x) {
        return (x & 2) == 0;
    }

    @Override
    public String toString() {
        return "  count " + count + "  min " + min +
            "  med " + median + "  max " + max +
            "  sum " + sum + "  mean " + mean +
            "  var " + var + "  sdev " + sdev;
    }
}
```

Programming Exercises

1. Copy the sum, mean, and meanStable functions as shown in this chapter into a Java class. Then write Java code that tests the mean and meanStable functions for the series of large numbers given in this chapter. What value does the mean function return? What value does the meanStable function return? Which answer is correct?
2. Write Java code to test the mean and meanStable functions with 10 random numbers in the range [1, 10]. Do both functions return the same answer?

A
Robust Code

There is an old computer programming joke that goes like this. A consultant went to a large company to teach the software engineers in the company. At the beginning of the class she said to the students, "If you got on an airplane and realized that your team had written the software that runs the airplane, how many of you would be afraid for your life and get off the plane?" Every student except one put his hand up. The consultant looked at the one student who didn't raise his hand and asked, "What does your team do differently so that you wouldn't be afraid to ride on the airplane?" The student answered, "Ha! if my team had written the software, the plane would never even get off the ground. I'd be perfectly safe."

Below are some programming practices that if you follow will make your software more robust (fewer errors) and help you rest easy on a working airplane for which you and your team wrote the software.

1. Follow generally accepted coding standards and conventions, including naming conventions.
2. Whenever possible, write simple, straight forward code. For example when writing in JavaScript, Java, C++, and C do not use the left shift operator (<<) to multiply by a power of two. Instead use multiplication (*) and rely on the compiler to generate fast code.
3. Minimize the number of execution paths through your code. (See the section Find a Range in chapter 1 of this book for an example of how to do this.)
4. Write each function to perform one and only one task.
5. Unless the function is extremely small and simple (ten lines of code or less), write each function with only one exit point (return statement).
6. When writing in a language that has exceptions, never return error codes from a function. Instead throw exceptions to indicate an error.
7. Turn on compiler warnings and never ignore them.
8. Write and use assertions. Test primarily with assertions turned on.
9. Write and execute unit tests and don't ignore test failures.
10. Consider writing a tricky algorithm twice, once with a straight forward, slow solution and once with a sophisticated, fast solution. In the debugging version of your program use the slow solution to verify the results of the fast solution.

Answers to Desk Checks

Chapter 1. Arrays

Desk Check 1.1 Fill

list

8.3	8.3	8.3	8.3
[0]	[1]	[2]	[3]

x
8.3

i
0
1
2
3
4

Desk Check 1.2 Ramp

list

0	1	2	3	4
[0]	[1]	[2]	[3]	[4]

i
0
1
2
3
4
5

Desk Check 1.3 Reverse Ramp

list

4	3	2	1	0
[0]	[1]	[2]	[3]	[4]

high
4

i
0
1
2
3
4
5

Desk Check 1.4 Reverse

list

~~3.4~~	~~−2~~	5	~~7~~	~~−12~~
12	7	5	−2	3.4
[0]	[1]	[2]	[3]	[4]

left	right	swap
0	4	3.4
1	3	−2
2	2	

Desk Check 1.5 Rotate Left

list

~~9~~	~~23~~	~~18~~	~~−3~~	~~8~~
23	18	−3	8	9
[0]	[1]	[2]	[3]	[4]

i	swap	last
0	9	4
1		
2		
3		
4		

Desk Check 1.6 Rotate Right

list

9	23	18	−3	8
8	9	23	18	−3
[0]	[1]	[2]	[3]	[4]

(top row values struck through)

i	last	swap
4	4	8
3		
2		
1		
0		

Desk Check 1.7 Rotate

list

11	23	−5	9	−3	14
−3	14	11	23	−5	9
[0]	[1]	[2]	[3]	[4]	[5]

(top row values struck through)

group	one	two	save
0	0	4	11
	4	2	
	2	0	
1	1	5	23
	5	3	
	3	1	
2			

k	n	groups
2	6	2
4		

Desk Check 1.8 gcd

a	b	r	return
2	6		2
2	6	2	
6	2	0	

Desk Check 1.9 printRotated

list

11	23	−5	9	−3	14
[0]	[1]	[2]	[3]	[4]	[5]

k	n	separator
2	6	""
		","

index	i	console output
−2		[−3,14,11,23,−5,9]
4		
5	0	
6	1	
0	2	
1	3	
2	4	
3	5	
4	6	

Desk Check 1.10 Linear Search

list

28.1	20	23.6	0	15
[0]	[1]	[2]	[3]	[4]

key	i	return
23.6	0	2
	1	
	2	

Desk Check 1.11 Binary Search

list

−2.1	−1	3.9	6.2	7.1	9.7	10	12	13.1	15.6	18	19	20.1	24.5
[0]	[1]	[2]	[3]	[4]	[5]	[6]	[7]	[8]	[9]	[10]	[11]	[12]	[13]

key	left	right	mid	cmp	return
15.6	0	13	6	5.6	9
	7		10	−2.4	
		9	8	2.5	
	9		9	0	

Desk Check 1.12 Find a Range

purchase	rate	discount	return
$708.00	0.025	17.7	690.3

Desk Check 1.13 Find a Range

purchase	rate	discount	return
$708.00	0.025	17.7	690.3

Desk Check 1.14 Find a Range

purchase	i	rate	discount	return
$708.00	0	0.025	17.7	690.3
	1			
	2			

Desk Check 1.17 Arabic to Roman

arabic	exponent	divisor	digit	roman
1987				""
987	3	1000	1	"M"
87	2	100	9	"MCM"
7	1	10	8	"MCMLXXX"
0	0	1	7	"MCMLXXXVII"

Desk Check 1.18 Roman to Arabic

roman	exponent	length	chars	digit	arabic
"MCMLXXXVII"					0
	3	4	"MCML"	−1	
		3	"MCM"	−1	
		2	"MC"	−1	
		1	"M"	1	1000
"CMLXXXVII"	2	4	"CMLX"	−1	
		3	"CML"	−1	
		2	"CM"	9	1900
"LXXXVII"	1	4	"LXXX"	8	1980
"VII"	0	4	"VII"	7	1987

Desk Check 1.20 Sort by Name or Age

students			console output
"Jane" 18	"Sam" 17	"Nigel" 14	[Jane 18, Sam 17, Nigel 14]
[0]	[1]	[2]	[Jane 18, Nigel 14, Sam 17]
			[Nigel 14, Sam 17, Jane 18]

Desk Check 1.21 Insertion Sort

list

6	-8	9	7	0
6	-8	9	0	7

6	-8	0	7	9

6	-8	0	7	9

-8	0	6	7	9
[0]	[1]	[2]	[3]	[4]

first	last	i	swap	j
0	4	3	7	4
				5
		2	9	3
				4
				5
		1	-8	2
		0	6	1
				2
				3
		-1		

Desk Check 1.22 findCandidates

candidates

"cash"	"charity"	"clothing"	"dentist"	"dividend"	"doctor"	"education"
[0]	[1]	[2]	[3]	[4]	[5]	[6]

prefix	index	first	last	bounds
"c"	1	1	1	null
		0	2	0, 2
		-1	3	
		0	2	

Desk Check 1.23 findAnyCandidate

candidates

"cash"	"charity"	"clothing"	"dentist"	"dividend"	"doctor"	"education"
[0]	[1]	[2]	[3]	[4]	[5]	[6]

prefix	left	mid	right	term	cmp	return
"c"	0	3	6	"dentist"	-1	1
		1	2	"charity"	0	

Desk Check 1.24 startsWithCompare

prefix	term	preLen	minLen	i	diff	return
"c"	"charity"	1	1	0	0	0
				1		

Desk Check 1.25 findBestCandidate

candidates

"cash"	"charity"	"clothing"	"dentist"	"dividend"	"doctor"	"education"
17	8	6	7	14	11	4
[0]	[1]	[2]	[3]	[4]	[5]	[6]

prefix	index	max	save	i	freq	return
"d"	3	7	3	2		4
				3		
	4	10		4	14	
				5	11	
				6		

Desk Check 1.26 findAnyCandidate

candidates

"cash"	"charity"	"clothing"	"dentist"	"dividend"	"doctor"	"education"
17	8	6	7	14	11	4
[0]	[1]	[2]	[3]	[4]	[5]	[6]

prefix	left	mid	right	term	cmp	return
"d"	0	3	6	"dentist"	0	3

Chapter 2. Array Lists

Desk Check 2.1 append

this.array

'U'	'n'	'd'	
[0]	[1]	[2]	[3]

this.count	c
2	'd'
3	

Desk Check 2.2 append

this.array

'U'	'n'	'd'	'a'	'u'	'n'		
[0]	[1]	[2]	[3]	[4]	[5]	[6]	[7]

this.count	i
3	0
4	1
5	2
6	3

a

'a'	'u'	'n'
[0]	[1]	[2]

Desk Check 2.3 append

this.array

'U'	'n'	'd'	'a'	'u'	'n'		
[0]	[1]	[2]	[3]	[4]	[5]	[6]	[7]

this.count	i
3	0
4	1
5	2
6	3

sb.array

'a'	'u'	'n'	
[0]	[1]	[2]	[3]

sb.count
3

Desk Check 2.4 append

this.array												this.count
'U'	'n'	'd'	'a'	'u'	'n'	't'	'e'	'd'				6
[0]	[1]	[2]	[3]	[4]	[5]	[6]	[7]	[8]	[9]	[10]	[11]	9

s	newLen
"ted"	9

Desk Check 2.5 expandCapacity

old				this.count	suggest	capacity
'U'	'n'	'd'		3	6	8
[0]	[1]	[2]	[3]			

this.array							
'U'	'n'	'd'					
[0]	[1]	[2]	[3]	[4]	[5]	[6]	[7]

Desk Check 2.6 findFibonacci

value	index	return
6	-2	8
	1	

Chapter 4. Iteration and Recursion

Desk Check 4.1 Iterative *n* factorial

n	fact
4	4
3	12
2	24
1	

Desk Check 4.2 Recursive *n* factorial

Function	Variables	
factorial	n	return
	4	24
factorial	n	return
	3	6
factorial	n	return
	2	2
factorial	n	return
	1	1

Desk Check 4.4 Iterative GCD

x	y	rem
472	24	16
24	16	8
16	8	0
8	0	

Desk Check 4.5 Recursive GCD

Function		Variables		
gcd	x	y	rem	return
	472	24	16	8
gcd	x	y	rem	return
	24	16	8	8
gcd	x	y	rem	return
	16	8	0	8

Desk Check 4.8 Recursive Sum

Function	Variables					
sum	a				return	
	6.5	7.1	6.9		20.5	
	[0]	[1]	[2]			
sumR				i	return	
				0	20.5	
sumR				i	return	
				1	14.0	
sumR				i	return	
				2	6.9	
sumR				i	return	
				3	0	

Desk Check 4.9 Tail Recursive Sum

Fucntion	Variables					
sum	a				return	
	6.5	7.1	6.9		20.5	
	[0]	[1]	[2]			
sumR			s	i	return	
			0	0	20.5	
sumR			s	i	return	
			6.5	1	20.5	
sumR			s	i	return	
			13.6	2	20.5	
sumR			s	i	return	
			20.5	3	20.5	

Desk Check 4.11 Tail Recursive *n* Factorial

Function   Variables

factorial

n	return
4	24

factorialR   f

f	n	return
1	4	24

factorialR

f	n	return
4	3	24

factorialR

f	n	return
12	2	24

factorialR

f	n	return
24	1	24

Desk Check 4.12 Recursive Pre-Order Traversal of a Binary Tree

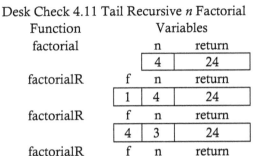

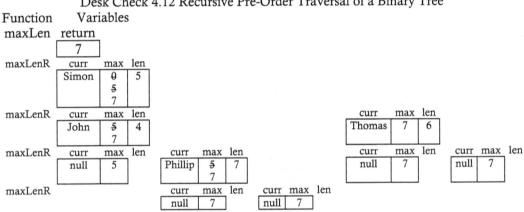

Function   Variables

maxLen   return

return
7

maxLenR   curr   max   len

curr	max	len
Simon	~~0~~ ~~5~~ 7	5

maxLenR   curr   max   len

curr	max	len
John	~~5~~ 7	4

maxLenR

curr	max	len
null	5	

curr	max	len
Phillip	~~5~~ 7	7

maxLenR

curr	max	len
null	7	

curr	max	len
null	7	

curr	max	len
Thomas	7	6

curr	max	len
null	7	

curr	max	len
null	7	

Desk Check 4.13 Iterative Pre-Order Traversal

stack   curr   len   max

Simon		

curr	len	max
		0
Simon	5	5

Thomas	John	

curr	len
John	4

Thomas	Phillip	null

curr	len	max
null		
Phillip	7	7

Thomas	null	null

curr	len
null	
null	
Thomas	6

null	null	
[0]	[1]	[2]

curr
null
null

Desk Check 4.14 Recursive In-Order Traversal

Function	Variables			
toList	list			
		John	Phillip	Simon	Thomas

Function	Variables		
toListR	curr		
	Simon		

toListR	curr		curr
	John		Thomas

toListR	curr	curr		curr	curr
	null	Phillip		null	null

toListR		curr	curr	
		null	null	

Desk Check 4.15 Iterative In-Order Traversal

list

John	Phillip	Simon	Thomas

stack		frame	
Simon, CheckLeft		node	todo
		Simon	CheckLeft
Simon, Process	John, CheckLeft		
		John	CheckLeft
Simon, Process	John, Process		
		John	Process
Simon, Process	Phillip, CheckLeft		
		Phillip	CheckLeft
Simon, Process	Phillip, Process		
		Phillip	Process
Simon, Process			
		Simon	Process
Thomas, CheckLeft			
		Thomas	CheckLeft
Thomas, Process			
		Thomas	Process

Desk Check 4.16 Recursive Fibonacci Function

Function	Variables					
fibonacci	n	return				
	4	3				

fibonacci	n	return			n	return
	2	1			3	2

fibonacci	n	return	n	return	n	return	n	return
	0	0	1	1	1	1	2	1

fibonacci							n	return	n	return
							0	0	1	1

Desk Check 4.17 Iterative Fibonacci Function

stack

```
| 4 |

| 3 | 2 |

| 3 | 1 | 0 |



| 2 | 1 |



| 1 | 0 |
 [0]   [1]   [2]   [3]
```

frame	n	fib
−1	4	0
0		
−1	4	
1		
0	2	
2		
1	0	
0	1	1
−1	3	
1		
0	1	2
−1	2	
1		
0	0	
−1	1	3

Desk Check 4.18 Iterative Fibonacci Function

future	past	present	n
	0	1	4
1	1	1	3
2	1	2	2
3	2	3	1
5	3	5	0

Desk Check 4.19 Tail Recursive Fibonacci Function

Function — Variables

fibonacci

n	return
4	3

fibonacciR

past	present	n	return
0	1	4	3

fibonacciR

past	present	n	return
1	1	3	3

fibonacciR

past	present	n	return
1	2	2	3

fibonacciR

past	present	n	return
2	3	1	3

fibonacciR

past	present	n	return
3	5	0	3

Desk Check 4.20 Fibonacci Formula

SQRT5	GOLDEN	n	numer	return
2.236	1.618	4	6.708	3

Desk Check 4.23 Iterative Binary Search

list

-2.1	-1	3.9	6.2	7.1	9.7	10	12	13.1	15.6	18	19	20.1	24.5
[0]	[1]	[2]	[3]	[4]	[5]	[6]	[7]	[8]	[9]	[10]	[11]	[12]	[13]

key	left	right	mid	cmp	return
15.6	0	13	6	5.6	9
	7		10	-2.4	
		9	8	2.5	
	9		9	0	

Desk Check 4.24 Recursive Binary Search

list

-2.1	-1	3.9	6.2	7.1	9.7	10	12	13.1	15.6	18	19	20.1	24.5
[0]	[1]	[2]	[3]	[4]	[5]	[6]	[7]	[8]	[9]	[10]	[11]	[12]	[13]

Function	Variables				
binarySearch	key	return			
	15.6	9			
binarySearchR	key	left	right	mid	cmp	return
	15.6	0	13	6	5.6	9
binarySearchR	key	left	right	mid	cmp	return
	15.6	7	13	10	-2.4	9
binarySearchR	key	left	right	mid	cmp	return
	15.6	7	9	8	2.5	9
binarySearchR	key	left	right	mid	cmp	return
	15.6	9	9	9	0	9

Desk Check 4.25 Future Value

principal	annualRate	years	periodsPerYear	rate	periods	fv
10000	0.06	2	4	0.005	8	11265

Desk Check 4.26 Iterative Future Value

i	principal	annualRate	years	periodsPerYear	rate	periods
	10000	0.06	2	4	0.005	8
1	10150					
2	10302					
3	10457					
4	10614					
5	10773					
6	10935					
7	11099					
8	11265					
9						

Function	Variables						
futureValue	principal	annualRate	years	periodsPerYear	rate	periods	return
	10000	0.06	2	4	0.005	8	11265
futureValueR	principal	rate	period	return			
	~~10000~~ 10150	0.005	~~8~~ 7	11265			
futureValueR	principal	rate	period	return			
	~~10150~~ 10302	0.005	~~7~~ 6	11265			
futureValueR	principal	rate	period	return			
	~~10302~~ 10457	0.005	~~6~~ 5	11265			
futureValueR	principal	rate	period	return			
	~~10457~~ 10614	0.005	~~5~~ 4	11265			
futureValueR	principal	rate	period	return			
	~~10614~~ 10773	0.005	~~4~~ 3	11265			
futureValueR	principal	rate	period	return			
	~~10773~~ 10935	0.005	~~3~~ 2	11265			
futureValueR	principal	rate	period	return			
	~~10935~~ 11099	0.005	~~2~~ 1	11265			
futureValueR	principal	rate	period	return			
	~~11099~~ 11265	0.005	~~1~~ 0	11265			
futureValueR	principal	rate	period	return			
	11265	0.005	~~0~~ −1	11265			

Chapter 5. Counting Bits

Desk Check 5.10 Shortcut Operators

	decimal	hexadecimal	binary
int x = 53;	53	00000035	0000 0000 0000 0000 0000 0000 0011 0101
x &= 0x0f;	5	00000005	0000 0000 0000 0000 0000 0000 0000 0101
x |= 0x70;	117	00000075	0000 0000 0000 0000 0000 0000 0111 0101
x ^= 0x6b;	30	0000001e	0000 0000 0000 0000 0000 0000 0001 1110
x <<= 2;	120	00000078	0000 0000 0000 0000 0000 0000 0111 1000
x >>>= 1;	60	0000003c	0000 0000 0000 0000 0000 0000 0011 1100
x >>= 1;	30	0000001e	0000 0000 0000 0000 0000 0000 0001 1110

Desk Check 5.11 Set and Clear Bits

	decimal	hexadecimal	binary
int x = 53;	53	00000035	0000 0000 0000 0000 0000 0000 0011 0101
1 << 3	8	00000008	0000 0000 0000 0000 0000 0000 0000 1000
x |= (1<<3);	61	0000003d	0000 0000 0000 0000 0000 0000 0011 1101
x & (1<<3)	8	00000008	0000 0000 0000 0000 0000 0000 0000 1000
~(1 << 3)	−9	fffffff7	1111 1111 1111 1111 1111 1111 1111 0111
x &= ~(1<<3);	53	00000035	0000 0000 0000 0000 0000 0000 0011 0101

Desk Check 5.12 Encrypt and Decrypt a Short Message

	hexadecimal	binary
plain	00007375 70657262	0000 0000 0000 0000 0111 0011 0111 0101 0111 0000 0110 0101 0111 0010 0110 0010
key	36a1804b e2f359e1	0011 0110 1010 0001 1000 0000 0100 1011 1110 0010 1111 0011 0101 1001 1110 0001
cipher	36a1f33e 92962b83	0011 0110 1010 0001 1111 0011 0011 1110 1001 0010 1001 0110 0010 1011 1000 0011
message	00007375 70657262	0000 0000 0000 0000 0111 0011 0111 0101 0111 0000 0110 0101 0111 0010 0110 0010

Desk Check 5.13 Swap Values

	decimal	hexadecimal	binary
int x = 53;	53	00000035	0000 0000 0000 0000 0000 0000 0011 0101
int y = -42;	−42	ffffffd6	1111 1111 1111 1111 1111 1111 1101 0110
x ^= y;	−29	ffffffe3	1111 1111 1111 1111 1111 1111 1110 0011
y ^= x;	53	00000035	0000 0000 0000 0000 0000 0000 0011 0101
x ^= y;	−42	ffffffd6	1111 1111 1111 1111 1111 1111 1101 0110

Desk Check 5.14 Naive

word	word & 1	n	i
		0	0
0011 0101	1	1	1
0001 1010	0		2
0000 1101	1	2	3
0000 0110	0		4
0000 0011	1	3	5
0000 0001	1	4	6
0000 0000	0		7
0000 0000	0		8

Desk Check 5.15 Loop Termination

word	word & 1	n
		0
0011 0101	1	1
0001 1010	0	
0000 1101	1	2
0000 0110	0	
0000 0011	1	3
0000 0001	1	4
0000 0000		

Desk Check 5.16 Addition

word	word & 1	n
		0
0011 0101	1	1
0001 1010	0	1
0000 1101	1	2
0000 0110	0	2
0000 0011	1	3
0000 0001	1	4
0000 0000		

Desk Check 5.17 Skip Zero Bits

word	n	word − 1
	0	
0011 0101	1	0011 0100
0011 0100	2	0011 0011
0011 0000	3	0010 1111
0010 0000	4	0001 1111
0000 0000		

Desk Check 5.18 Combinatorial

word	word >>> 1	ones	word >>> 1 & ones	word & ones
0011 0101	0001 1010	0101 0101	0001 0000	0001 0101

word >>> 2	twos	word >>> 2 & twos	word & twos
0010 0101	0000 1001	0011 0011	0000 0001	0010 0001

word >>> 4	(word >>> 4) + word	fours
0010 0010	0000 0010	0010 0100	0000 1111

0000 0100

Desk Check 5.19 Lookup

word	(int)word & 0xff	onbits[(int)word & 0xff]
0011 0101	0011 0101	4

Chapter 6. Sets

Desk Check 6.1 Naive Contains

array

"apple"	"pear"	"plum"	"cherry"	"peach"
[0]	[1]	[2]	[3]	[4]

term	i	return
"plum"	0	true
	1	
	2	

Desk Check 6.2 Naive Is Subset

this

"elm"	"pine"	"rose"
[0]	[1]	[2]

setB

"lilac"	"pine"	"fir"	"elm"
[0]	[1]	[2]	[3]

i	termA	return
0	"elm"	false
1	"pine"	
2	"rose"	
3		

Desk Check 6.3 Naive Intersection

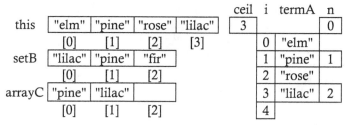

this

"elm"	"pine"	"rose"	"lilac"
[0]	[1]	[2]	[3]

setB

"lilac"	"pine"	"fir"
[0]	[1]	[2]

arrayC

"pine"	"lilac"	
[0]	[1]	[2]

ceil	i	termA	n
3			0
	0	"elm"	
	1	"pine"	1
	2	"rose"	
	3	"lilac"	2
	4		

Desk Check 6.4 Naive Relative Complement

this

"elm"	"pine"	"rose"	"lilac"
[0]	[1]	[2]	[3]

setB

"lilac"	"pine"	"fir"
[0]	[1]	[2]

arrayC

"elm"	"rose"		
[0]	[1]	[2]	[3]

ceil	i	termA	n
4			0
	0	"elm"	1
	1	"pine"	
	2	"rose"	2
	3	"lilac"	
	4		

Desk Check 6.5 Naive Union

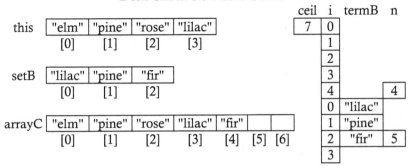

this

"elm"	"pine"	"rose"	"lilac"
[0]	[1]	[2]	[3]

setB

"lilac"	"pine"	"fir"
[0]	[1]	[2]

arrayC

"elm"	"pine"	"rose"	"lilac"	"fir"		
[0]	[1]	[2]	[3]	[4]	[5]	[6]

ceil	i	termB	n
7	0		
	1		
	2		
	3		
	4		4
	0	"lilac"	
	1	"pine"	
	2	"fir"	5
	3		

Desk Check 6.6 Merge Is Subset

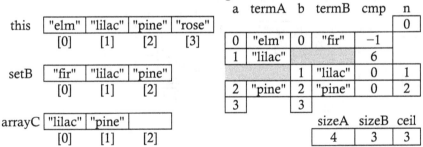

this

"elm"	"pine"	"rose"
[0]	[1]	[2]

setB

"elm"	"fir"	"lilac"	"pine"
[0]	[1]	[2]	[3]

sizeA	sizeB	a	b	cmp	return
3	4	0	0	0	false
		1	1	10	
		2	4		
		3	0		
		2	4		

Desk Check 6.7 Merge Intersection

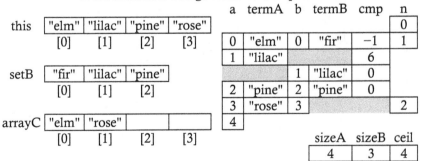

this

"elm"	"lilac"	"pine"	"rose"
[0]	[1]	[2]	[3]

setB

"fir"	"lilac"	"pine"
[0]	[1]	[2]

arrayC

"lilac"	"pine"	
[0]	[1]	[2]

a	termA	b	termB	cmp	n
					0
0	"elm"	0	"fir"	−1	
1	"lilac"			6	
		1	"lilac"	0	1
2	"pine"	2	"pine"	0	2
3		3			

sizeA	sizeB	ceil
4	3	3

Desk Check 6.8 Merge Relative Complement

this

"elm"	"lilac"	"pine"	"rose"
[0]	[1]	[2]	[3]

setB

"fir"	"lilac"	"pine"
[0]	[1]	[2]

arrayC

"elm"	"rose"		
[0]	[1]	[2]	[3]

a	termA	b	termB	cmp	n
					0
0	"elm"	0	"fir"	−1	1
1	"lilac"			6	
		1	"lilac"	0	
2	"pine"	2	"pine"	0	
3	"rose"	3			2
4					

sizeA	sizeB	ceil
4	3	4

Desk Check 6.9 Merge Union

	"elm"	"lilac"	"pine"	"rose"
this				
	[0]	[1]	[2]	[3]

	"fir"	"lilac"	"pine"
setB			
	[0]	[1]	[2]

sizeA	sizeB	ceil
4	3	7

	a	termA	b	termB	cmp	n
						0
	0	"elm"	0	"fir"	−1	1
	1	"lilac"			6	2
			1	"lilac"	0	3
	2	"pine"	2	"pine"	0	4
	3	"rose"	3			5
	4					

	"elm"	"fir"	"lilac"	"pine"	"rose"		
arrayC							
	[0]	[1]	[2]	[3]	[4]	[5]	[6]

Desk Check 6.10 Bitset Add

universe.list

"elm"	"pine"	"rose"	"lilac"	"fir"			
[0]	[1]	[2]	[3]	[4]	[5]	[6]	[7]

bitset	term	index	found	i	return
0101 0000	"fir"	null	false	4	true
0101 1000					

Desk Check 6.11 Bitset Remove

universe.list

"elm"	"pine"	"rose"	"lilac"	"fir"	"ash"		
[0]	[1]	[2]	[3]	[4]	[5]	[6]	[7]

bitset	term	index	i	found	return
1101 1000	"pine"	1	1	false	true
1001 1000				true	

Desk Check 6.12 Bitset Contains

universe.list

"elm"	"pine"	"rose"	"lilac"	"fir"	"ash"		
[0]	[1]	[2]	[3]	[4]	[5]	[6]	[7]

bitset	term	index	found
1101 1000	"lilac"	3	true

Desk Check 6.13 Bitset Is Subset

universe.list

"elm"	"pine"	"rose"	"lilac"	"fir"	"ash"		
[0]	[1]	[2]	[3]	[4]	[5]	[6]	[7]

this.bitset	setB.bitset	temp	return
1110 000	1101 1000	1110 0000	false
		1100 0000	

Desk Check 6.14 Bitset Intersection

universe.list

"elm"	"pine"	"rose"	"lilac"	"fir"	"ash"		
[0]	[1]	[2]	[3]	[4]	[5]	[6]	[7]

this.bitset	setB.bitset	result.bitset
1110 0000	1101 1000	1110 0000
		1100 0000

Desk Check 6.15 Bitset Relative Complement

universe.list

"elm"	"pine"	"rose"	"lilac"	"fir"	"ash"		
[0]	[1]	[2]	[3]	[4]	[5]	[6]	[7]

this.bitset	setB.bitset	result.bitset
1110 0000	1101 1000	1110 0000
		0010 0000

Desk Check 6.16 Bitset Union

universe.list

"elm"	"pine"	"rose"	"lilac"	"fir"	"ash"		
[0]	[1]	[2]	[3]	[4]	[5]	[6]	[7]

this.bitset	setB.bitset	result.bitset
1110 0000	1101 1000	1110 0000
		1111 1000

Advanced Programming Techniques

Chapter 7. Statistics

Desk Check 7.1 Minimum

data					i	min
9	12.3	−3	5			9
[0]	[1]	[2]	[3]		1	
					2	−3
					3	
					4	

Desk Check 7.2 Sum

data					i	s
7	3	−2	4.4			0
[0]	[1]	[2]	[3]		0	7
					1	10
					2	8
					3	12.4
					4	

Desk Check 7.3 Sum

data					x	s
7	3	−2	4.4			0
[0]	[1]	[2]	[3]		7	7
					3	10
					−2	8
					4.4	12.4

Desk Check 7.4 Mean

data				s	return
7	3	−2	4.4	12.4	3.1
[0]	[1]	[2]	[3]		

Desk Check 7.5 Two Pass Variance

data				m	i	x	t	sqsum	var
7	3	−2	4.4	3.1				0	10.73
[0]	[1]	[2]	[3]		0	7	3.9	15.21	
					1	3	−0.1	15.22	
					2	−2	−5.1	41.23	
					3	4.4	1.3	42.92	
					4				

Desk Check 7.6 One Pass Variance

data

7	3	-2	4.4
[0]	[1]	[2]	[3]

i	x	sum	sqsum	n	mean	var
		0	0	4	3.1	10.73
0	7	7	49			
1	3	10	58			
2	-2	8	62			
3	4.4	12.4	81.36			

Desk Check 7.7 One Pass Correlation

dataX

12	4	3.9	2.1
[0]	[1]	[2]	[3]

dataY

12	3.2	3.5	1.9
[0]	[1]	[2]	[3]

i	x	y	sumX	sumY	sumX2	sumY2	sumXY
			0	0	0	0	0
0	12	12	12	12	144	144	144
1	4	3.2	16	15.2	160	154.24	156.8
2	3.9	3.5	19.9	18.7	175.21	166.49	170.45
3	2.1	1.9	22	20.6	179.62	170.1	174.44
4							

n	meanX	meanY	sdevX	sdevY	covar	correl
4	5.5	5.15	3.83	4.00	15.29	0.998

Desk Check 7.8 Stable Mean

data

-2	3	4.4	7
[0]	[1]	[2]	[3]

i	delta	mean
		-2
1	5	0.5
2	3.9	1.8
3	5.2	3.1

Desk Check 7.9 Stable Variance

data

-2	3	4.4	7
[0]	[1]	[2]	[3]

i	weight	delta	mean	sqsum	var
			-2	0	10.73
1	0.5	5	0.5	12.5	
2	0.67	3.9	1.8	22.64	
3	0.75	5.2	3.1	42.92	
4					

Desk Check 7.11 Multiple Statistics

data

-2	3	4.4	7
[0]	[1]	[2]	[3]

i	x	weight	delta	mean	sqsum
				-2	0
1	3	0.5	5	0.5	12.5
2	4.4	0.67	3.9	1.8	22.64
3	7	0.75	5.2	3.1	42.92
4					

count	min	med	max	sum	var	sdev
4	-2	3.7	7	12.4	10.73	3.28

Index

& (address-of operator), 42

& (bitwise and), 76

^ (bitwise exclusive or), 77

| (bitwise or), 76

~ (bitwise not), 76, 77

<< (left shift), 73, 115

>> (signed right shift), 74

>>> (unsigned right shift), 9, 74

array, 1
   binary search. *See* binary search
   element, 1
   fill, 1
   index, 1
   linear search, 7
   ramp, 2
   reverse, 3
   rotate, 4
   sort, 15, 17
   subscript, 1

array list, 25
   capacity, 25
   doubling, 26
   Fibonacci, 27
   initial capacity, 25
   quantum, 25
   size, 25

assert, 115

binary search, 7, 68

binary search tree, 44, 58, 60

bitset, 73, 95
   add, 96
   contains, 97
   equals, 97
   intersect, 98
   relative complement, 98
   remove, 96
   size, 96
   subset, 97
   union, 98

bitwise operators, 73
   and (&), 76
   exclusive or (^), 77
   left shift (<<), 73, 115
   not (~), 76
   or (|), 76
   signed right shift (>>), 74
   unsigned right shift (>>>), 9, 74

Boolean, 73

compound growth, 70

correlation coefficient. *See* statistics

cyclomatic complexity, 49

desk check, vii

divide by a power of two, 74

Erlang, 52

factorial, 51, 57

Fibonacci series, 27, 31, 62

floating point arithmetic, 108

for each loop, 102

future value, 70

golden ratio, 64

greatest common divisor, 5, 54

Haskell, 52

input
   possible user input, 18
   predictive user input, 21

iteration, 51, 72
   converting to recursion, 68

java.lang
   Long, 83
   String, 18
   StringBuffer, 25, 26
   StringBuilder, 25, 26, 28